MARIANO
RIVERA

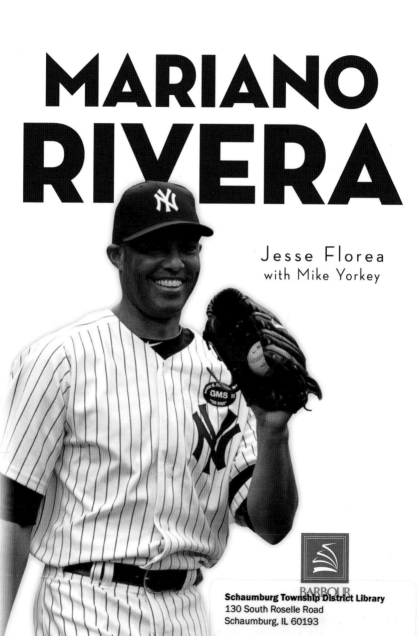

Jesse Florea
with Mike Yorkey

BARBOUR

© 2013 by Jesse Florea and Mike Yorkey

Print ISBN 978-1-62029-821-3

eBook Editions:
Adobe Digital Edition (.epub) 978-1-62029-999-9
Kindle and MobiPocket Edition (.prc) 978-1-62029-998-2

The authors are represented by WordServe Literary Group, Ltd., Greg Johnson, Literary Agent,
10152 S. Knoll Circle, Highlands Ranch, CO 80130

Published by Barbour Publishing, Inc., P.O. Box 719, Uhrichsville, Ohio 44683,
www.barbourbooks.com

*Our mission is to publish and distribute inspirational products offering exceptional value and biblical
encouragement to the masses.*

 Member of the
Evangelical Christian
Publishers Association

Printed in the United States of America.

CONTENTS

1
THIRTEEN PITCHES
TO HISTORY

Heading into the 2011 season, the question wasn't *if* New York Yankee pitcher Mariano Rivera was the best closer in Major League Baseball history but *when* he'd break the all-time saves record and prove that fact.

The answer to that question came on September 19 at Yankee Stadium. The Yankees held a 6–4 lead over the Minnesota Twins heading into the top of the ninth inning. Like the team had done so many times over the previous sixteen seasons, New York called on Mariano to clinch the victory.

Throughout the game, the Yankees faithful could feel something special in the air. The electricity had built as New York clung to a two-run lead after six innings. Mariano had come into the game with 601 saves, tying him for the all-time lead with San Diego Padres great Trevor Hoffman.

The Bronx pulsated with energy as the innings went by. The crowd erupted with cheers when New York's Nick Swisher grounded into an inning-ending double play in the eighth—not because the fans wanted Swisher to fail but because the end of the eighth meant it was time for Mariano to go for the record.

The crowd grew even louder between innings as Mariano jogged from the bullpen to the mound and took his warm-up pitches.

"Let's go, Mo!" fans chanted.

Moments later, the cheering ratcheted up another level as Trevor Plouffe, the Twins' second hitter, stepped into the batter's box to lead off the ninth inning. It wasn't going to be easy for Mariano to pick up his 602nd save. He'd have to go through the heart of Minnesota's lineup, which included Michael Cuddyer and Chris Parmelee—both of whom had hit home runs earlier in the game.

The situation. The noise. The pressure. None of it seemed to rattle Mariano. He stared steel-eyed at his catcher, Russell Martin, gritted his teeth, and delivered his first pitch. Four pitches later, Plouffe found himself sitting on the bench after hitting a harmless ground ball to second base. Cuddyer suffered a similar fate. On a two-and-two count, he hit a lazy fly ball to right field for the second out.

That brought up Parmelee. Mariano kicked and delivered a belt-high pitch on the outside edge of the plate. *Strike one.* The Yankee crowd began a deafening chant of "Mar-i-a-no!" Parmelee managed to make contact with the second pitch, fouling off an inside pitch and breaking his bat in the process. *Strike two.* As Parmelee walked back to the dugout to grab some new wood, the crowd's excitement grew. Back in the batter's box, with new lumber in his hands, Parmelee could only watch as Mariano's signature cut fastball hit 93 miles per hour and caught the outside corner of home plate. *Strike three!*

Three pitches. Three strikes. One historic out.

In all, Mariano threw thirteen pitches to retire the Twins in 1-2-3 order.

Yankees fans and players jumped around with excitement. Mariano simply smiled, hugged Martin, and took the game ball from his catcher. After Mariano hugged his fellow Yankees— including all the relief pitchers, who had run in from the bullpen— long-time teammate Jorge Posada nudged Mariano back onto the mound to accept the fans' adulation.

"For the first time in my career, I'm on the mound alone," Mariano said later. "It was priceless. I didn't know it could be like that."

Mariano blew a kiss to the Yankee Stadium faithful and took off his hat to thank the fans who had cheered for him since he entered the major leagues. He smiled and threw up his arms, looking almost embarrassed at all the applause.

After several moments, Mariano rejoined his teammates and walked off the field. Immediately following the game, reporters surrounded Mariano and asked what it felt like to be the best closer of all time.

Like he'd done countless times in the past, Mariano deflected the attention from himself and put the focus on his teammates—and on God.

"The whole organization, my whole teammates have been a pillar for me," Mariano told reporters. "I always have to talk about God because that's the most important thing in my life. Yes, there have been bumps in the road, but God gave me the strength."

God's strength almost seems to flow through Mariano on the mound. At 6 feet, 2 inches tall and 195 pounds, he's not an imposing figure with the ball in his hand. But once the ball leaves his fingers, the pitch seems to explode toward the plate.

The Yankee closer always credits God with his success. For years, he has written his favorite Bible verse, Philippians 4:13, on his baseball glove: "I can do everything through him who gives me strength."

Mariano's words and actions after setting the saves record only added to his reputation as one of the kindest and humblest players ever to lace up a pair of cleats.

Everybody seemed happy for him. Even after losing, many of the Twins stayed in the dugout and on the field to help honor Mariano's accomplishment. And Trevor Hoffman, now in second place on the all-time saves list, offered his best wishes.

"I want to congratulate Mariano Rivera on setting the all-time saves record," Hoffman said in a statement. "It's a great accomplishment, and he is still going strong! I have tremendous respect for Mariano not just for his on-field accomplishments, but also for his service to the community."

Between the time he came up with the Yankees in 1995 and the end of the 2012 season, Mariano had earned 608 saves. Only he and Hoffman have passed the 600 mark . . . and that doesn't count Mariano's 42 postseason saves, which are also a major league record. When he's on the mound, the Yankees nearly always secure a victory. His save percentage is a hair under 90 percent—the best ever for pitchers with 250 or more opportunities.

How Does a Pitcher Earn a Save?

1. He finishes a game won by his team.
2. He does not receive the win.
3. He meets one of the following three criteria:
   a. Enters the game with a lead of no more than three runs and pitches at least one inning.
   b. Enters the game with the tying run either on base, at bat, or on deck.
   c. Pitches effectively for at least the last three innings.

In the playoffs, where things *really* matter, Mariano has been nearly unhittable. He has helped New York win five World Series titles and was named the Most Valuable Player of the 1999 Fall Classic.

Only twenty-one pitchers in baseball history have tallied *half* the number of saves this slender hurler, known as the "Hammer of God," has earned. Mariano has won the American League Rolaids Relief Man Award five times and has been voted an All-Star twelve times.

Despite the accolades and accomplishments, Mariano stays humble and firmly rooted in his Christian faith. He lets his actions, instead of his words, do the talking.

When asked if being called the greatest closer of all time embarrasses him, Mariano answered: "Yes, it does. It does make me uncomfortable because I don't like to talk about myself. I just want to be able to contribute as much as I can for the team. And the rest is just blessings from the Lord."

The Lord has blessed Mariano with a long career, a beautiful family, and numerous records. Those are things many players would get a big head about. Not Mariano.

"I'm thankful to my wife, my kids, my family, the organization, my teammates," Mariano explains. "That's what I'm thankful for, for where God has put me and for what God has done for my life—and that involves everything. More than proud, I'm thankful."

And that spirit of thankfulness carries Mariano through the good times and the bad—like those he experienced at the beginning of the 2012 season.

2
WARNING TRACK MISHAP

Every team enters a baseball season with hope. Everybody is filled with excitement when pitchers and catchers show up for spring training in the middle of February. After a gloomy winter, baseball season bursts out with a promise of rebirth and sunnier times.

Players know that anything can happen within the course of a 162-game season. There will be slumps and winning streaks, pennant races, and underdog stories. For example, who could've guessed that the Washington Nationals would go from National League East basement dwellers in 2010 to having the best record in baseball two years later?

The New York Yankees, like they almost always seem to do, entered the 2012 campaign as the favorites to win the American League East. During the off-season, they'd added Raul Ibanez's big bat and acquired two new starting pitchers—Hiroki Kuroda

Mariano Rivera pitched brilliantly for the Yankees during the 2011 American League Divisional Series against Detroit, but the Tigers still claimed the series three games to two. (Tomasso DeRosa/ Four Seam Images via AP Images)

and Michael Pineda. Add to that the return of Yankee great Andy Pettitte and Yankee fans already dreamed of their team's twenty-eighth World Series title. Those dreams were a lot sweeter than the memories from the previous fall.

As the top seed in the American League, the Yankees drew the Detroit Tigers in a best-of-five 2011 divisional series. The Bronx Bombers played like the best in their opening game, beating the Tigers 9–3. Two straight victories by Detroit struck fear in the Yankee faithful, but after New York rebounded for a 10–1 victory in Game 4, fans were certain the Yankees would pull out the deciding win at Yankee Stadium. Those hopes were dashed, however, when the Tigers gritted out a 3–2 victory to advance to the American League Championship Series.

The Yankees' season was over. Mariano pitched well in his two appearances, even lowering his earned run average in the playoffs to an unheard of 0.70. But because his team either won by a lot or lost close games, Mariano wasn't able to add to his major league–leading 42 postseason saves.

But hope springs eternal, especially when it's spring and you're wearing Yankee pinstripes.

New York began the season near its spring training headquarters in Florida. Right out of the gate, the Yankees tested their mettle against the powerful Tampa Bay Rays. With the lead after eight innings, manager Joe Girardi called on Mariano to ice the victory. For his career, Mariano had converted 60 of 61 save chances against the Rays. However, Tampa thrilled the home crowd with a win by plating two runs in a ninth-inning rally.

Mariano had blown his first save opportunity of the 2012 season. But less than a month later, the Yankee hurler had regained his regular form to notch five saves and post a 1–1 record. Then, during a sunny afternoon in Kansas City, Missouri, the unthinkable happened. The greatest closer of all time found himself crumpled on the warning track at Kauffman Stadium after injuring his right knee.

No, Mariano didn't trip coming out of the bullpen. Just like he's recognized for shutting down teams at the end of games, Mariano is known for chasing down fly balls before the contest ever begins.

The game against the Royals in early May started out like any other during Mariano's eighteen years with the Yankees. The players arrived at the ballpark a few hours early, changed into warm-ups, and headed out for batting practice. Because American League pitchers don't bat—due to the designated hitter rule—Mariano traditionally stations himself in center field to run down fly balls.

During batting practice, pitchers usually have the duty of rounding up balls—and Mariano attacks the job with passion. While other players jog to pick up balls or stand at the fence talking, Mariano sprints around the outfield catching everything he can get to. The right-hander had played in the outfield growing up in Panama and even asked Girardi if he could play center field during a game before he retired.

Girardi wanted to grant Mariano his wish of playing in the outfield but worried about the All-Star getting hurt during the

Unusual Outfielders

Mariano Rivera isn't the only great pitcher known for racing around the outfield shagging fly balls.

The legendary Atlanta Braves pitching staff of Greg Maddux, Tom Glavine, John Smoltz, Denny Neagle, and Steve Avery often found themselves showing off their glove skills before games. Arguably one of the best rotations in major league history, these players helped the Braves win their division year after year in the 1990s. Atlanta even claimed the 1995 World Series title.

These pitchers had incredible talent, pinpoint accuracy, and great velocity, but more than anything they possessed a competitive drive. They competed in everything—wins, strikeouts, hitting home runs in batting practice, even a game called "500" before actual games.

While the rest of the Braves would usually stand near buckets of baseballs talking and barely paying attention during batting practice, Smoltz, Neagle, and the others would sprint around the outfield catching fly balls. A catch in the air was worth 100 points. A one-hopper scored fewer points. The first one to 500 points won . . . and they *all* wanted to win.

game. But, as the Yankees found out, a manager can't always control injuries.

Before the game on May 3, Mariano had chased down a ball in center field, leaping for it as he reached the warning track. Landing awkwardly on his right leg, the forty-two-year-old took a quick hop on his left leg before crashing into the wall. He immediately grabbed his right knee, fell to the ground, and writhed in pain. Teammates in blue and gray uniforms looked worried as they stared at their bullpen anchor lying in the dirt.

All-Star third baseman Alex Rodriguez watched the events transpire as he waited near home plate for his turn to bat. As Mariano went down, A-Rod immediately called to manager Joe Girardi, who ran to center field to check on his closer.

"He's been [chasing fly balls] and no one ever said a word," Girardi said. "That's part of who he is. You take that away from him, and he may not be the same guy, the same pitcher."

Mariano was helped from the field, put on a cart, and taken to Kansas University Med West hospital for a magnetic resonance imaging test. The diagnosis wasn't good: a torn anterior cruciate ligament (ACL) and a damaged meniscus. The ACL is one of the four major ligaments in the knee. It stabilizes the knee and keeps the shinbone properly aligned with the thighbone. As a right-handed pitcher, Mariano pushes off using his right leg, so his right knee must be strong for him to have power behind his pitches.

Mariano returned to the Yankee locker room after the game to face questions from reporters. The next day, newspapers and websites published headlines saying that the injury might force Mariano into retirement. CAREER MAY BE OVER read a headline in the *New York Times*.

Watching the scene and hearing Mariano speak after the game, it was hard to argue with that assessment.

"I got myself between the grass and the dirt, couldn't pull my leg up, and twisted my knee," he explained. "If it's going to happen like that, at least it happened doing what I love to do. I love shagging balls. If I had it to do all over again, I'd do it again. No hesitations."

Mariano spoke deliberately, but when one reporter asked how his injury would affect the Yankees, he choked up.

"Feel like I let the team down," he said, holding back tears.

His reaction proves what fans already knew: Mariano loves the Yankees and is a team-first player.

After Mariano first learned the diagnosis, he wondered if he'd ever pitch again.

"At this point I don't know," he said in the press conference. "It all depends how the rehab is going to happen."

But a day later, Mariano had changed his tune.

"I'm coming back," he told reporters. "Write it down in big letters. I'm not going out like this."

Mariano didn't want to end his career sitting in the dirt on a warning track. His legacy is much greater than that. He had *defined* his position as closer. He was the picture of consistency. And he had developed possibly the most devastating pitch in baseball history.

3
A PITCH THAT'S A CUT ABOVE

Playing catch. Fathers do it with their sons and daughters. Little Leaguers do it to warm up before a game. Even major league players do it to stay in shape and work on their mechanics.

But during a routine game of catch with teammate Ramiro Mendoza in June 1997, Mariano couldn't get his throws to go straight. Every time he threw the ball, it would cut and move at the last moment. Mendoza, a fellow pitcher, had trouble even catching the ball.

Mendoza told Mariano to cut it out, but Mariano couldn't. The ball just seemed naturally to move that way.

Mariano had always like fiddling with how he held the baseball. His long fingers and flexible wrist were perfect for a pitcher. But now he had a problem . . . or did he?

At the time, Mariano had been with the Yankees for only a couple of seasons. He got batters out with a four-seam fastball

Mariano Rivera's consistent delivery and devastating cut fastball show up even when he's throwing batting practice—here, before a Yankees spring training game at Steinbrenner Field in 2010. (AP Photo/Kathy Willens)

that he threw with great velocity and accuracy. Sometimes Mariano's fastball had good movement, but sometimes it came toward the plate straighter.

Now he didn't know where his pitches would end up. Mariano told Mendoza that he thought he was holding the ball the same way. The movement was unexplainable.

Today Mariano has an explanation for the amazing cutting action on his fastball. "That is my miracle pitch," Mariano says. "That's what I call it, because it's God's gifting. I didn't have that pitch before, and nobody taught me that. It came as a miracle."

Later in June, Mariano still had difficulty throwing the ball straight as he warmed up before entering a game against the Detroit Tigers. Yankee bullpen catcher Mike Borzello had never seen a pitch like this. It looked like a fastball at first, but then it started a wicked darting action about five feet before reaching the plate. Even the experienced catcher had difficulty keeping the ball from getting past him.

Mariano pitched that night and recorded the save. He converted his next three save opportunities as well.

At first, Yankees pitching coach Mel Stottlemyre tried to help Mariano remove the cutting action from his pitches. For a month, Stottlemyre and Borzello worked with Mariano on his grip and release.

"We were trying to make the pitch stay straighter, [as it had] in '95 and '96," Mariano says. "But it didn't work. Then I said, 'I'm tired of working at this. Let's let it happen.' "

What happened was that Mariano now possessed a pitch

that looked like a fastball but acted like a slider when it got close to the plate. Well, sort of. A slider generally moves *downward*, but Mariano's pitch moved *sideways*. And it didn't take Mariano long to perfect precision with his signature cut fastball. He controlled its location by putting different pressure on the ball with his fingertips. Greater pressure with his middle finger made it move one way. Using the index finger a little more caused it to react differently.

From a hitter's perspective, Mariano's delivery looked effortless. But in an instant, the ball exploded to the plate at nearly 95 miles per hour.

Jim Thome, who as of the end of the 2012 season has hit more than 600 home runs in his major league career, called Mariano's cut fastball the greatest pitch in baseball history. Longtime Minnesota Twins manager Tom Kelly once said, "[Mariano] needs to pitch in a higher league, if there is one. Ban him from baseball. He should be illegal."

How to Throw the Cut Fastball

Mariano Rivera didn't invent the cut fastball. He simply perfected it. Nobody knows who threw the first cutter. Now every pitcher wants to throw one.

"When I broke in [to the majors in 1999], I could count on one hand the number of guys who threw it," veteran outfielder Lance Berkman said. "Now it's like I can count on one hand the guys who *don't* have it."

Pitching coach Gil Patterson has helped many pitchers learn the basics of the cutter. He even taught it to Roy

Halladay, and it quickly became the Cy Young Award winner's most devastating pitch. (Halladay throws his cut fastball about 20 percent of the time.)

Patterson says the grip for a cutter is nearly identical to that of a four-seam fastball; however, pitchers must move the grip slightly off center and then squeeze hard with their middle finger as they release the ball.

While a slider tends to break downward, a cutter moves sideways, which is why batters often hit the pitch off their hands or near the end of the bat.

If you want to learn how to throw the cut fastball, search the Internet for "How to Throw a Cut Fastball Like Mariano Rivera." A video and description of the pitch will show you the basics. Then it's up to you to practice and experiment until you can make it work like a pro.

Scientists have studied thousands of Mariano's pitches. What makes him so difficult to hit is that he throws the cut fastball and four-seam fastball with the exact same motion and release. His hand stays behind the ball, and his fingers rest on top. He never turns or flicks his wrist like other pitchers do to create the spin for a slider or curveball.

"Look at Mo's delivery, look at how he repeats it," marveled Joba Chamberlain, who joined the Yankees in 2007. "He does the same exact thing every time. That's a very hard thing to do—I try, but I can't do it like Mo. There's never any added stress on his arm because all the parts move the same way every time."

Contrary to popular belief, big league batters don't possess supernatural reflexes and reaction speeds. What allows a batter to hit a ball are visual cues from the pitcher's arm and tons of practice. If a pitcher drops down in his delivery or flicks his wrist, a batter can anticipate where the ball is going to be when it reaches the plate.

Batters have only about a tenth of a second—that's how long it takes to blink your eyes—to determine what kind of pitch they see and if they want to swing.

"You can't see the spin on [Mariano's cutter]," six-time All Star Lance Berkman said. "A four-seam fastball rotates a certain way. A slider or a cutter is going to spin a certain way—you see a red dot on the ball as it's coming at you from the seams as it spins. And once you see the rotation on it, you react a certain way. The good cutters, like Rivera's, rotate like a four-seamer—you don't see the red dot, you don't know it's going to come in on you until it's too late."

When Mariano is on the mound, batters often think they're seeing a hittable pitch coming over the plate. But by the time they make contact, the ball has moved several inches and is either in on their hands or hit off the end of the bat. Rarely do hitters make contact with the fat part of the bat. More times than not, the ball hits near their hands and often ends up breaking the bat. Mariano has unofficially led the major leagues in broken bats every year since he developed his cut fastball. Some sportscasters have joked that bat maker Louisville Slugger should pay Mariano a bonus because of all the business he's brought its way.

But this pitch is no joke to Mariano—it's a blessing.

Mariano Rivera and Yankee catcher Jorge Posada (left) got to know each other so well—both on and off the field—that Posada sometimes wouldn't flash signs to tell Mariano what pitch to throw. He just knew what was coming. (AP Photo/Julie Jacobson)

"I'm a thousand percent. A thousand percent sure," Mariano says. "[It's] just a gift from the Lord."

Since mastering the pitch, Mariano throws his cut fastball more than 90 percent of the time. He might mix in an occasional two-seam fastball, and about four times a year, he'll throw a changeup just to keep batters honest.

Once Jorge Posada became the Yankees' everyday catcher, it got to the point where he didn't flash signs to tell Mariano what pitch to throw. Posada would simply signal to throw the pitch over the inside or outside *corner* of the plate. Mariano rarely throws one down the middle. With pinpoint accuracy and a determination to win, Mariano goes after the black edges of the plate.

And unlike a lot of closers, Mariano doesn't resort to intimidation. He doesn't believe in throwing brushback pitches—one, because he isn't out there to show up hitters, and two, because that would waste a pitch. All Mariano wants to do is throw strikes.

"My mental approach is simple: Get three outs as quick as possible," he says. "If I can throw three, four pitches, the better it is. I don't care how I get you out, as long as I get you out."

Mariano may not try to intimidate hitters when he enters the game, but he does possess four characteristics every closer needs to succeed.

4
THE FOUR C'S OF CLOSING

Almost everything about Mariano is the opposite of what most people think of when they picture a relief pitcher. Closers tend to be a high-strung bunch, known for their bushy beards, waxed moustaches, big rope necklaces, nervous tics, and unpredictable behavior on the mound.

If Mariano could be described in one word, it would be *predictable*. He warms up the same way before every appearance. He never looks rushed or worried. His demeanor is always calm, whether he's pitching in a spring training game or in the World Series. Even his signature pitch—the cut fastball—is predictable. Batters know it's coming, but they still can't hit it.

The Yankees know they can always count on Mariano. Before his injury at the beginning of the 2012 season, he'd been as reliable as the sun rising in the east. Since taking over as the full-time closer in New York in 1997, Mariano has provided amazing stability in the Yankee bullpen.

Although Mariano's actions may not line up with the craziness associated with most relief pitchers, he does possess four *other* C's that every closer needs to succeed: confidence, concentration, control, and competitiveness.

• **Confidence.** Every time Mariano walks onto the field, a Yankee victory hangs in the balance. If he does his job, the Yankees win. If he struggles, all of his team's hard work from the previous eight innings could be erased. It's a pressure-packed situation with all eyes in the stadium focused on him.

But Mariano doesn't fear the pressure—he embraces it.

"If the pressure is so much that it doesn't allow you to do your job, then that kind of pressure is bad," Mariano says. "But if you don't think about it and just go out and do your job, you can have success."

Mariano has had plenty of success. More than 90 percent of the time he's called on to close a game, he notches a save and secures a Yankee victory. Sometimes, however, the other team is able to get some hits and score a run against him. In all of his years in New York, he's never blown more than nine save opportunities in a season. Every blown save hurts, but he doesn't let it shake his confidence.

"If I doubted myself, I wouldn't be doing this," Mariano says. "You just go out and do it. That's the mind-set that a closer has to have."

Instead of dwelling on a blown save, he looks at it as an opportunity to improve. "I don't call them blown saves," Mariano says. "I call them learning processes. I learn when I do something wrong and then try to move on."

Much of Mariano's confidence comes from years of success on the mound. But his greatest source of confidence comes from his Lord, Jesus Christ.

"When God takes control of everything, He's inside of you and He brings you strength," Mariano says. "He has the power to do everything for you. I feel like God is on my side and will help me deal with anything."

• **Concentration.** One of the first bits of advice Little League coaches give pitchers is to focus on the target. They want their young pitchers to concentrate on one thing: the catcher's glove.

Mariano takes that focus to another level. His laserlike concentration allows him to block out everything—fans cheering and chanting his name, hecklers from the crowd, organ music— and throw perfect strikes. Friends have often come to Yankee games and tried to get Mariano's attention when he's on the mound. Some have even been a little offended because he seems to be ignoring them. But Mariano's not ignoring his friends—he just doesn't see them.

When Mariano digs his cleats into the pitcher's mound, he enters his own little world.

"I feel like it's just me and the catcher," Mariano says. "I don't even see the hitter. I feel like everything is gone—the noise, the fans. I'm in kind of like a tube, and it's the catcher and me."

Mariano says the pitcher's mound is a peaceful place for him, even a place of worship.

Mariano Rivera doesn't show a lot of emotion on the mound, but he couldn't help but smile after breaking Major League Baseball's all-time saves record at the end of the 2011 season. (AP Photo/Kathy Kmonicek)

"Every time before I throw my first pitch, I am praying," he says. "And not only that, in the bullpen I am praying. I know there are millions of people praying for me, and I strongly believe in prayers."

• **Control.** Relief pitchers don't have time to mess around on the mound. Every pitch counts. They can't afford to walk batters and put potential tying runs on base. Pinpoint control is a must.

The average major league pitcher throws a strike 62 percent of the time. But according to 2009 statistics, nearly 70 percent of Mariano's pitches are strikes. And his strikes aren't down the fat part of the plate. He paints the corners with his cut fastball and makes it difficult for batters to get solid wood on the ball.

Mariano doesn't just control his pitches on the mound—he also controls his emotions.

"I don't get nervous," Mariano says. "I trust God. If I get nervous, I can't do my job."

• **Competitiveness.** Mariano may look calm and composed on the mound, but he's fiercely competitive. He wants to win at everything he does—a trait he possessed even as a small child.

"Since I was a little one, I was real competitive," Mariano says. "I never give up. If you beat me, you have to beat me one, three, four, five times, and I still don't give up."

That competitive drive helped him develop his cut fastball. He worked hard at it, throwing it over and over again until he had it mastered. He knew it was a weapon that would help the Yankees win a lot of games. And Mariano always wants the Yankees to win.

During the early innings of games, Mariano can often be found in the clubhouse watching the game on TV. He'll shout at the television screen and cheer on his teammates.

"He's a trip in here during the game—screaming, yelling, cheering, rooting," says former Yankee pitcher A.J. Burnett. "It's loud. I mean, he's shouting, 'Come on, you can do it!' He's yelling at the TV and jumping around."

Mariano sometimes gets so caught up in the game that his competitiveness spills out onto the field. During an August 2011 game against the Kansas City Royals, Mariano watched as the umpires got a home run call wrong. After seeing the replay on TV, he ran from the clubhouse to the dugout to complain about the call.

Once Mariano actually steps on the field, all of that jumping around is gone. He focuses his competitive energies on one thing: getting three outs as quickly as he can.

"I love everything about pitching," Mariano says. "Just being on the mound and competing. There is nobody to come and save you. You have to get it done. There is no time to play around. It's time to get it done and go home."

Today Mariano makes his home in a New York City suburb. But he grew up about 3,000 miles from the bright lights of Yankee Stadium, in a small Panamanian fishing village.

The History of "Firemen"

For nearly a hundred years, there was no such thing as a closing pitcher in baseball. The "save" didn't become an official Major League Baseball statistic until 1969. Not long after, teams started to develop pitchers who would throw the last few innings of a game to clinch a victory.

At first, these pitchers were called "firemen" because they'd often enter the game to put out an offensive "fire" from the other team. A manager would call for his fireman when the opponent already had runners on base and was threatening to score.

In the 1970s, pitchers such as Rollie Fingers, Bruce Sutter, and Rich "Goose" Gossage gained fame with their abilities to come out of the bullpen and shut down opponents. They'd regularly pitch several innings in relief. In fact, for their careers, Gossage and Sutter have more saves of two innings or more than one-inning saves.

The role of the modern-day closing pitcher didn't truly develop until the early 1990s. Manager Tony La Russa, who has won World Series titles with the Oakland A's and with the St. Louis Cardinals, made Dennis Eckersley the first pitcher to be used nearly exclusively in the ninth inning.

Today's closers almost always pitch just one inning a game. For his career, Mariano Rivera has just one save of seven outs or more, while Gossage (who also pitched for the Yankees) notched 53.

As of the beginning of the 2012 season, only five closing pitchers have ever been inducted to baseball's Hall of Fame: Eckersley, Fingers, Gossage, Sutter, and Hoyt Wilhelm (a knuckleball thrower from 1952–72 who specialized in relief pitching).

5
REAL-LIFE FISH STORY

Puerto Caimito is a tightly knit coastal fishing village in central Panama. People who live in this tiny town on the Gulf of Panama have always made their living from the sea—mainly through fishing. Everybody there knows everybody, and everybody knows that the most famous person to come from their village is Mariano Rivera.

Mariano was born on November 29, 1969, in Panama's capital of Panama City, about thirty-five miles away from Puerto Caimito. The son of a fisherman, he lived in a house that sat about a hundred feet from the ocean. But don't get a mental picture of a luxurious beach home. Many houses in this area consist of concrete blocks and corrugated tin roofs.

"My childhood was wonderful," Mariano says. "Oh, man. I didn't have much. Basically, I didn't have anything. But what we had, I was happy."

When Mariano closes his eyes, he can still picture his boyhood home. White sand. Cool ocean breezes. The land dotted with mango trees. Gentle, friendly people.

The Rivera home often felt pretty cramped for Mariano and his three siblings. (He has an older sister and two younger brothers.) So Mariano spent a lot of time outdoors.

His sport of choice as a child was soccer, but he also played baseball . . . if you count using a stick to hit a ball made of electrical tape wrapped around fish netting as baseball.

Sports Panama-Style

The country of Panama bridges Central and South America. It's best known for the Panama Canal, which allows ships to sail between the Atlantic and Pacific Oceans without having to go all the way around the southern tip of the continent of South America. But it's also well-known for its sports.

Many sports that are popular in the United States share similar popularity in Panama. Although soccer (called *fútbol* in Panama) is the most popular sport, Panamanian children also enjoy basketball and baseball, and there are professional leagues for all of these sports. Boxing, tennis, and golf also enjoy a high level of popularity in Panama.

Because Panama borders two huge bodies of water and is only about the size of South Carolina, water sports are immensely popular. Snorkeling, fishing, scuba diving, surfing, and beach volleyball are all favorites for locals and visitors.

During his early elementary school years, Mariano and his friends would make a ball, cut a few straight tree branches to use as bats, and fashion gloves and chest protectors out of cardboard. Then they'd wait for low tide. Games could be played in the streets, but that could sometimes be dangerous. Besides, a wide stretch of sand during low tide made a much better playing field. But even then, games brought an element of danger.

Mariano remembers one particular baseball game with his cousins (almost everybody on the two teams was related). One cousin threw a fastball that another cousin fouled back. A third cousin, who was playing catcher without a mask, took the foul ball right below the eye. The welt ballooned up about the size of a baseball.

Sometimes one of the boys would get an actual baseball for Christmas or for his birthday. But it wouldn't take long before the aggressive swings and constant use would tear the cover off the ball. Mariano says tennis balls were a luxury—and not very durable. The boys in Puerto Caimito would hit the balls so hard that they would quickly rip.

When Mariano was twelve, his father bought him a real leather baseball glove. The youngster was so excited that he slept with the glove and took it everywhere with him, even to school.

Mariano's father worked hard as a fisherman, earning around $50 a week, to provide for his four children. His catch of the day often made its way to the dinner table. He was also a strict disciplinarian. Mariano remembers receiving a lot of spankings, but he knew his father punished him for his own good.

As Mariano entered Pablo Sanchez High School, he dreamed of becoming a professional soccer player. He had quick feet and a smooth athleticism. What he *didn't* have, however, was the ability to stay healthy. Numerous ankle injuries caused him to give up on his *fútbol* aspirations.

Instead of bending it like Beckham, Mariano went fishing like his father—and many of the other men in his village. Panamanian fishermen throw nets in the cool Pacific Ocean to catch sardines, snapper, herring, grouper, and other fish.

Following his graduation from high school at the age of sixteen, Mariano went into the family business. He wasn't afraid of hard work, but after a few years of working with his father, he realized fishing wasn't for him. The boats would go out for six days a week. Everybody slept onboard. If enough fish weren't caught during the day, they'd fish at night—even in the rain. Mariano often found himself untangling nets or helping to pull in the lines to drag hundreds of pounds of fish into the boat.

And sometimes fishing was dangerous, especially during high seas. At the age of nineteen, Mariano was aboard a 120-ton fishing boat when it started to capsize. The motor stopped working, and the boat began taking on water. Mariano and the rest of the crew had to flee for their lives. Fortunately, everyone made it to the safety of a nearby boat.

Mariano admits that was a scary experience, but everything about being a fisherman was hard. "Extremely hard," he says. "I wanted to study to be a mechanic. Obviously, I didn't do it because the Lord had different plans for me."

While Mariano didn't follow his father's footsteps into fishing, he did pick up a lot from Mariano Sr.—including his strong character and generous spirit. If his father could help someone, he would, Mariano says—even if that meant giving a person his last $10. (Panama uses the American dollar as its currency.) Plus, his father is willing to work hard.

"From my father's side, I got the strength, the mental toughness, the heart, the courage," Mariano says.

But the Yankee great also credits his mother's side of the family for making him into the person he is today. He spent a lot of time with his grandfather on his mother's side, who would cut trees in the *manglares*, a junglelike mangrove habitat. Mariano saw the patience he demonstrated and the attention to detail.

"The piece of my mother I have [is] the gentleness, the worries, making sure everybody is okay," he says about his mother, Delia.

That willingness to help and put others above himself ultimately helped open the door for Mariano to make it to the major leagues. Because while he enjoyed playing baseball growing up, he didn't want to be a pitcher—until he had to be.

6
FROM *VAQUEROS* TO PINSTRIPES

What is it about kids and rocks? When the two of them get together, one is bound to get thrown—and it won't be the kids!

Thousands of stones dotted beaches around Puerto Caimito, and kids would often throw them into the ocean, at trees, or toward signs. Mariano Rivera was an excellent rock thrower growing up. He had uncanny aim—it seemed like he could hit anything with a rock in his hand.

Of course, when it came to sports, Mariano preferred using his feet over his arm. He had great speed on the soccer field and on the baseball diamond. So even though he could throw, he liked to play in the field. He enjoyed using his quickness and strong arm at shortstop, and he could use his running ability in the outfield.

After Mariano determined that fishing wasn't his life's passion, he joined a local amateur baseball team. The eighteen-year-old looked good sporting the green and gold uniform of *Panamá Oeste* (Panama West).

In nearby South American countries, soccer is king. But Panama, Nicaragua, Puerto Rico, the Dominican Republic, and other Latin American countries have a long history in baseball. Major League teams, always looking for untapped talent outside the U.S. border, send scouts throughout Latin America hoping they can discover players who have the skills to play at the big league level.

Numerous regional teams in Panama give athletes an opportunity to continue working on their baseball skills after high school. Over the years, dozens of Panamanian players have played in the majors. For example, Rod Carew, one of the best hitters ever, played in the majors from 1967 to 1985 and was the first Panamanian player inducted into the Baseball Hall of Fame.

America's Pastime

Baseball has long been called "America's pastime." Based on the British sport "rounders," modern baseball was invented in the United States in the mid-1800s. Since then, the sport has become a key part of U.S. history. Baseball has a much shorter history in Latin America, but it has shown amazing growth since the 1980s.

In 1990, about 13 percent of major league players were from Latin America. Now that number is around 30 percent. The tiny island nation of the Dominican Republic alone produces nearly one out of every ten players who plays in the big leagues.

PLAYING WITH PURPOSE: MARIANO RIVERA

At the beginning of the 2011 major league season, eighty-six players hailed from the Dominican Republic, sixty-two from Venezuela, twenty from Puerto Rico, and four (including Mariano Rivera) from Panama. And Mariano is far from the only Latin American player to make a big name for himself.

Albert Pujols, whom many consider the best first baseman ever to play the game, moved from the Dominican Republic to the United States as a teenager. And Miguel Cabrera, who grew up in Venezuela, won baseball's Triple Crown in 2012. That means he led the American League in batting average (.330), home runs (44), and RBI (139). He was just the thirteenth player in major league history to accomplish the feat, the first to do it in forty-five years, and the first Latin American player to win the award.

"As a scout, you're signing players to get to the big leagues, not Double-A or Triple-A," said longtime scout Herb Raybourn.

Raybourn, who was born and raised in Panama, often attended Panama's national baseball tournament. He first saw Mariano play in 1988, when the *Vaqueros* (Cowboys) made it all the way to the finals.

At 6 feet, 2 inches tall and weighing 155 pounds, Mariano made an impact as a rangy shortstop with a good arm. His batting stroke, however, was less than impressive.

"I gave him good marks in his fielding and throwing," Raybourn said. "But his hitting was questionable. I just didn't think that he'd be able to hit that well in the big leagues."

Raybourn passed on Mariano, as did all the other professional scouts.

A year later, *Panamá Oeste* again qualified for the national tournament. After a long season, the *Vaqueros* pitching staff was pretty beat up. Some pitchers were plagued by injuries, while others would get lit up every time they took the ball.

Mariano didn't like losing. His competitive spirit drove him to do whatever it took to win, even if that meant pitching.

During one game, Mariano was in the outfield and his team's best pitcher was getting bombed. No other pitchers were available, so Mariano volunteered to step onto the mound. He had thrown some growing up and was always good at hurling rocks at a target, so maybe he could help the team win as a pitcher. The *Vaqueros* ended up coming from behind to win the game, and the team ended up with a new pitcher.

Two weeks later, Mariano was returning from the beach with his parents and girlfriend, Clara, when two teammates ran up to him. Catcher Claudino Hernandez and center fielder Emilio Gaez said they'd found him a tryout with the New York Yankees.

Mariano wasn't overpowering as a pitcher, but he was accurate. So accurate, in fact, that Chico Heron, a Yankees scout, noticed him. Heron set up a tryout with Raybourn, who the previous year had become the head of Latin American scouting for the Yankees.

Mariano traveled to Panama City for the audition. Raybourn immediately recognized him. The skinny shortstop took the ball and walked to the mound.

Mariano remembers the tryout like it happened yesterday. "I wasn't nervous," he says. "I had nothing to lose."

He had thrown just nine pitches—all of which registered in the mid-80s on the radar gun—when Raybourn stopped him. Mariano thought he'd blown it. Big league pitchers typically throw in the 90s—and some even top 100 miles per hour with their fastball. But Raybourn had seen enough.

"The radar wasn't really being lit up," Raybourn says. "But what I liked about Mariano was his looseness, a nice loose arm. And his fastball had a lot of movement. I could picture him pitching in the majors."

Raybourn figured that with some professional coaching and weight training, Mariano could gain some extra zip on his fastball. Raybourn also thought Mariano could learn a few other pitches.

On February 17, 1990, the twenty-year-old signed with the Yankees and received a $3,500 signing bonus. The Atlanta Braves drafted Chipper Jones No. 1 overall that same year and gave him a $252,000 bonus—nearly a quarter million dollars more than Mariano received.

Mariano couldn't have been more excited, however. Before he inked the contract, he had never seriously thought about playing professional baseball. But now he was no longer a *Vaquero*; he would wear the pinstripes of the New York Yankees.

"Usually a player prepares for years [for this]," Mariano says. "Here I was signing, and I wasn't even a pitcher."

Mariano's excitement was also tempered with fear. He had

never traveled far from his home. He didn't even speak English. Plus, he'd have to leave his family, his friends, and his girlfriend. He cried when he left Puerto Caimito. So did his mother.

The road to the major leagues wouldn't be easy, and Mariano knew it. But he had no idea about the amazing help that he was about to receive.

7
FISHER OF MEN

Mariano boarded a plane and flew to Tampa, Florida, to join the Gulf Coast League Yankees. Tampa may sit next to the water and be home to numerous white, sandy beaches, but that's where the similarities between it and Puerto Caimito stop. Instead of small fishing boats and a quiet lifestyle, Tampa featured huge cruise ships and a busy nightlife. Plus, everybody spoke English.

Mariano missed home.

"My first year when I was in Tampa and my second year in North Carolina, it was no English," Mariano says. "I cried because I couldn't communicate with my teammates, with my pitching coordinator, my manager—I was frustrated."

Because there were no phones at his parents' house in Panama, Mariano mailed them letters. Sometimes weeks would go by without Mariano's mother hearing anything from her oldest son. She worried about him. She knew he was lonely and living in a strange place.

Mariano may have felt like he didn't fit in off the field, but he looked at home on it. The Gulf Coast League was for rookies who weren't ready for Class A ball. Many of the players came straight out of high school or were in situations similar to Mariano's—athletes who had been scouted and signed from another country.

Mariano no longer showed his range at shortstop or played in the outfield. The Yankees signed him to be a pitcher. While Mariano still didn't feel like a pitcher, he threw like one. In 22 games, he pitched 52 innings and gave up one earned run while striking out 58 and walking just 7.

On the last day of the Gulf Coast League season, the Yankee manager asked him to pitch on just two days rest. Typically, pitchers need four or five days' rest to recover from a start and get their arm strength back. But Mariano didn't hesitate. He took the ball and pitched seven innings of no-hit, shutout baseball. The Yankees were already seeing that Mariano had the ability to bounce back quickly and pitch at his best.

In 1991, Mariano advanced to the Class A Greensboro (North Carolina) Hornets. While his record (4–9) was subpar, he posted an impressive 2.75 earned run average and a 123-to-36 strikeouts-to-walk ratio.

But 1991's greatest highlights for Mariano occurred off the field, not on it. First, he dedicated himself that year to learning English. None of his Hornet teammates spoke Spanish, so he asked them to teach him the right way to speak his new language.

Then, following his year in North Carolina, Mariano flew home and married his longtime girlfriend, Clara. They had known each other since elementary school. It was the perfect example of two friends deciding to make a lifelong commitment to each other. They exchanged vows on November 9, 1991.

In the spring of 1992, the magazine *Baseball America* ranked Mariano as the ninth-best Yankee prospect. Derek Jeter was rated second, just ahead of Andy Pettitte. The Yankees bumped up Mariano to their top Class A team in Fort Lauderdale, Florida.

Again, he pitched well as a starter. He posted a 5–3 record with a 2.28 earned run average. His strikeouts dropped to 42, but he allowed a paltry five walks. Still, Mariano knew that a mid-80s fastball and decent changeup wouldn't get him promoted to the majors. He started trying to develop a curve ball by snapping his wrist to create more spin. But the experiment proved to be painful and unsuccessful. The change in his throwing mechanics put extra stress on his elbow and wrist. On August 27, 1992, before the season was over, Mariano went in for elbow surgery.

Elbow surgery can end a pitcher's career. At first, surgeons thought they'd have to replace a ligament in Mariano's arm. But during the surgery, they determined that the ligament could be repaired. That made his recovery much quicker, and by the start of spring training in 1993, he was ready to continue his career.

Mariano began the 1993 season back in the Gulf Coast League but quickly advanced to Greensboro. His manager with the Hornets, Brian Butterfield, loved Mariano's attitude and baseball skills.

"This guy is our best outfielder," Butterfield said, describing the way Mariano tracked down balls during batting practice. He certainly wasn't the Hornets best shortstop. By this time, Derek Jeter and Mariano were teammates. The two future Yankee greats quickly became friends.

"After Mo had surgery, when we were in the minor leagues, he was on a pitch count," Jeter remembers. "So I used to count his pitches at short for him. I'd go to the mound and tell him he was wasting too many pitches. True story."

Mariano's statistics were again impressive but not noteworthy enough to move him up in the Yankee farm system. That happened in 1994.

Mariano began the year with New York's high-level Class A team in Tampa. After posting a 3–0 record, he moved to the Double-A Albany-Colonie Yankees. A month and a half later, he made his debut with the Triple-A Columbus Clippers. He started six games at Columbus and had a 4–2 record. However, his 5.81 ERA worried the Yankee higher-ups. Mariano had a big league attitude and athleticism, but his pitches still lacked pop.

He suffered a setback in the beginning of August when he strained a hamstring and couldn't pitch for ten days. It was one of many obstacles Mariano had to overcome during his days in the minor leagues.

Unlike big league players, who get paid millions of dollars and travel to games on jets, minor league players struggle to get by financially and often have to take long bus trips.

Mariano made between $500 and $800 a month in the minor leagues, definitely not enough to raise a growing family—especially when sickness or other emergencies came up. In the midst of all

Mariano Rivera has known Joe Girardi, right, as his catcher, friend, and manager throughout most of his Yankee career. (AP Photo/John Dunn)

his adversities in 1994, Mariano made a life-changing decision: he prayed to accept Jesus Christ as his Savior.

"Every time I was going through a hard time, somebody was there to help," Mariano says. "It's not too often when you play in the minor leagues that a coach will tell you he will take care of your son while you stay with your wife at the hospital. My pitching coach did that. And one lady in Panama, who I didn't know before, offered to stay with my wife while I was playing. Even though I had nobody here, I was never alone. That made me accept Jesus as my Savior. I knew it wasn't a coincidence. It was the Lord putting someone there for me."

Mariano had determined years before that he didn't want to be a fisherman, but now he was firmly committed to becoming—as Jesus put it in Matthew 4:19—a fisher of men.

"I realized the Lord wanted a relationship with me," he says. "That's when I became a Christian."

Mariano's decision to follow the Lord didn't come overnight. It was thoughtful. He couldn't ignore God's obvious work in his life. As God's Word says in Romans 1:19–20, "For what can be known about God is plain to them, because God has shown it to them. For his invisible attributes, namely, his eternal power and divine nature, have been clearly perceived" (ESV).

Time and time again, God showed up for him. Sometimes Mariano saw God work through the kindness of other people; other times it was God Himself working out different circumstances for him.

But in 1995, God did something for Mariano he never could have imagined.

Getting Saved

God doesn't only want a relationship with great baseball players; He wants a relationship with you. The Bible says Jesus died for everybody's sins and wants all people to accept His saving love.

Have you ever made a decision to follow Jesus Christ? Mariano Rivera was twenty-four years old when he prayed to invite Jesus into his life. It's never too late to give your life to Christ. He loves you unconditionally and is always ready to forgive you.

Maybe you've seen God's love demonstrated to you in personal ways. Many centuries ago, Jesus died so your sins could be forgiven and you could live with Him forever in heaven. All you have to do is open your heart and accept His free gift of forgiveness.

If you'd like to begin a personal relationship with Jesus, just pray something like this:

Jesus, I've done some bad things. I believe You took the punishment for my sins on the cross so I could be forgiven. Thank You for dying for me and rising from the dead. I accept Your gift of salvation and ask You to be the Lord of my life. Help me to follow You. Amen.

If you just prayed this prayer, tell your parents, a family member, or a pastor. Then get yourself a Bible so you can learn about God and grow closer to Him. Discovering more about God's saving grace is a lifelong journey.

8
THE NEED FOR SPEED

The 1995 season couldn't have started out much better for Mariano Rivera . . . and the rest of Major League Baseball. That was a good thing, because 1994 was a year to forget.

On August 12, 1994, the owners locked out the players and the players went on strike. The Players Association and Major League Baseball couldn't agree to a new contract that would get teams back on the field. The strike lasted 232 days—the longest in baseball history—and led to the cancellation of the rest of the 1994 season, including the World Series. It was the first time since 1904 that baseball hadn't crowned a champion.

But on March 31, 1995, Judge Sonia Sotomayor—now a U.S. Supreme Court justice—issued an injunction stating that it was unfair of the owners to lock out the players. Two days later, the players went back to work. The 1995 season was shortened from the usual 162 games to 144 games—after an abbreviated spring training.

The season began on April 24, but Mariano started the year back in Columbus. Less than a month later, several Yankees pitchers were injured, opening a door for the twenty-five-year-old starter. Clipper manager Bill Evers called Mariano and told him that he'd been called up to the big leagues. Mariano had just finished pitching a game in Rhode Island when Evers phoned him in his hotel room. At first, he didn't believe his coach. But when he realized that it wasn't a joke (it was nowhere near April Fool's Day), he jumped up and down on his hotel bed and then called his family in Panama.

Then it was just a short trip to New York City. Mariano made his debut with the Bronx Bombers against the California Angels. The Angels greeted Mo in a way that was anything but angelic. They roughed up the starter by notching eight hits and five runs before Mariano was taken out of the game in the fourth inning.

It wasn't an opening night disaster, but it didn't help Mariano's chances of staying in New York for long. Three additional starts for the Yankees didn't go much better. He posted a 10.20 earned run average and was quickly sent back to Columbus.

The Yankees still liked Mariano, but his 87-mph fastball didn't wow big league hitters. His changeup was good, and his delivery fooled some batters. He had potential, but New York fans expect their team to win *now*. The Yankees needed help in the starting pitching rotation, so they contacted the Detroit Tigers about a possible trade for David Wells. (Wells compiled a 239–157 record in the majors before retiring in 2007.) Detroit wanted Mariano in return, and Yankees general manager Gene Michael thought about pulling the trigger on the deal.

Mariano Rivera became a mainstay on the Yankees pitching staff in 1996, but he didn't become New York's closer until a season later. (AP Photo/Kathy Willens)

Now That's a Fastball

Mariano Rivera's mid-eighties fastball didn't amaze anyone. These fastballs do:

- Texas pitcher Nolan Ryan was known as the "Ryan Express." One of his flame-throwing fastballs reached 108.1 mph, according to Doppler laser radar readings in 1974.

- It's not just modern-day pitchers who bring the heat. Hall of Famer Bob Feller threw a 107.6-mph fastball for the Cleveland Indians in 1946.

- On April 18, 2011, Cincinnati Reds pitcher Aroldis Chapman threw a pitch that registered 106 mph on the radar gun at the Great American Ballpark. Another gun clocked it at 105. Either way, it's one of the fastest pitches ever thrown during a major league game—and the fastest recorded with modern radar guns, which were introduced in the 1980s.

- Detroit closer Joel Zumaya fired a 104.8-mph fastball in 2006. Hand, elbow, and shoulder injuries later plagued his major league career.

- Mark Wohlers brought the heat for the Atlanta Braves in 1995. That's when he threw a 103-mph fastball. He also earned 25 saves that year.

- Many pitchers have thrown 102 mph, but not when they're forty years old. That's what Randy Johnson did in 2004 as a starter for the Arizona Diamondbacks.

- Closers often reach back to hurl an occasional 102-mph fastball. Detroit Tigers starter Justin Verlander consistently brings 100-mph heat, including 102-mph fastballs.

Then, on June 26, 1995, two weeks after Mariano was sent back to the minors, something amazing happened—his fastball got faster. A *lot* faster.

Mariano pitched five no-hit innings against the Rochester Red Wings. Jorge Posada, the catcher for Columbus at the time, said batters didn't have a chance as the radar gun consistently clocked Mo's pitches at 95 miles per hour.

Where did the additional 10 miles per hour come from? Michael saw the report and didn't believe it. The Yankee GM called Evers to ask if the speed gun was broken. When he found out Mariano was now throwing in the mid-90s, all trade talks ended. Mariano would stay a Yankee.

But that still left the question about the source of the extra speed. Nobody could explain it. Since moving to the United States, Mariano had added twenty-five pounds of muscle by working out and eating right. It had been more than two and a half years since his elbow surgery. But why now? How did the burst of speed just materialize in two weeks?

Mariano had an answer: it was a gift from God. And it was a gift that would keep on giving.

The extra oomph on his fastball earned Mariano a return trip to New York. This time he fared much better. On July 4, 1995, he struck out 11 in eight shutout innings of work against the Chicago White Sox. He was with the Yankees to stay.

New York finished the season with a 79–65 record. It was Major League Baseball's first season of expanded (four teams per league) playoffs, so New York qualified for the postseason as the wild card.

Mariano made the postseason roster as a middle reliever. The Yankees faced Seattle in the first round. At the time, the Mariners had an impressive lineup that included Ken Griffey Jr., Tino Martinez, Mike Blowers, and Edgar Martinez. Plus they had Randy Johnson on the mound.

The Yankees surprised the American League West champions by beating them in the first two games of the best-of-five series. Mariano earned the victory in Game 2 by pitching three-plus innings of scoreless ball in extra innings. New York finally won the game 7–5 in the fifteenth inning. The Mariners came back to win the series three games to two, but Mariano pitched well each time he was given the opportunity. In Game 3, he recorded four outs without giving up a hit.

Then he entered the deciding fifth game in the eighth inning with the game tied and the bases loaded. The hard-hitting Blowers stood at the plate. Even with limited big league experience, Mariano looked calm. He struck out Blowers on three pitches. He got an additional out in the ninth inning before being taken out of the game. The Yankees went on to lose in eleven innings.

In all, Mariano faced 16 batters in the postseason and had a 0.00 earned run average.

"I know what people were probably thinking then," Mariano says. "Who is this guy?"

Nobody knew who he was at the time. But his performance in the playoffs provided a glimpse of who Mariano would become in the future.

9
ENTER THE SANDMAN

First you hear the guitar. A cymbal keeps the beat. Soon, hard-driving drums kick in. Then more guitars join the fray and jam this heavy metal tune into full force.

As soon as the first strains of Metallica's "Enter Sandman" ooze out of the Yankee Stadium sound system, the song gets overwhelmed by cheering fans. The heavy metal anthem and New York closer Mariano Rivera are linked. Some people even nicknamed Mariano "The Sandman," because once he enters the game, it's lights out for the other team.

Although the Yankees didn't use "Enter Sandman" as Mariano's entrance music until 1999, he pitched a lights-out season in New York in 1996.

By this time, the Yankees were loaded with young talent, including Jorge Posada, Derek Jeter, Andy Pettitte, and Bernie Williams.

The Yankees have had plenty of reasons to celebrate since Mariano Rivera (at far right, No. 42) joined Major League Baseball's winningest team. The normally reserved pitcher never misses an opportunity to celebrate with his teammates. (AP Photo/Dick Druckman)

Welcome to the Music

Before "Enter Sandman" became Mariano Rivera's official entrance music, the Yankees tried two Guns N' Roses songs. But the fans didn't react to "Paradise City" or "Welcome to the Jungle."

Then Mike Luzzi, a freelance member of the scoreboard crew, brought in a personal copy of one of his favorite Metallica CDs. The fans went crazy when they played the first track from that disc as Mariano entered the game.

Four years passed before Mariano knew the lyrics to "Enter Sandman." He doesn't dislike the song; it's just not his preferred musical style.

"I didn't pick that song," Mariano says. "I didn't know Metallica or 'Enter Sandman.' They chose it, and we stick with it . . . . I listen to Christian music."

Mariano doesn't have a favorite Christian song. And he's okay with "Enter Sandman" being played when he enters a game because the fans enjoy it so much.

Once Mariano retires, so will the song—at least as far as entrance music at Yankee Stadium is concerned. According to Michael Bonner, the Yankees' senior director of scoreboard and broadcasting: "After Mo is done, we won't use that for anyone else. It's meant for the greatest of all time."

Joe Torre had taken over as manager. With enough starting pitching on the roster, Torre knew he wanted to use Mariano as a reliever . . . he just didn't know the exact role Mariano would play.

The Yankees soon figured out that Mariano was the perfect setup man for closer John Wetteland. With Mariano and Wetteland coming out of the bullpen that year, the Yankees notched an amazing 79–1 record in games in which they held a lead after seven innings.

New York recorded a 92–70 regular season record—tops in the American League East. It was the Yankees' first division title since 1981, a fifteen-year drought. And Mariano and Wetteland had a lot to do with the success. Basically, if the Bronx Bombers held a lead in the seventh inning, they were going to win. Mariano would pitch an inning or two then give the ball to Wetteland.

For the season, Mariano struck out 130 batters in 107.2 innings of work. Wetteland pitched just 63.2 innings to amass 43 saves.

Speaking of saves, on May 17, 1996, Mariano earned his first after inducing a game-ending double play against the California Angels. After the save, he smiled, laughed, and high-fived teammates.

The Yankees would do plenty more high-fiving that season.

The Yankees had failed to win a World Series since 1978, but they rolled into the 1996 playoffs. They lost the first game of the American League Divisional Series against Texas but then roared back to win three straight and take the series. In the American League Championship Series, New York beat Baltimore four games to one. Mariano picked up the victory in Game 1, pitching two scoreless innings as the Yankees won 5–4 in eleven innings.

In the World Series, the boys in pinstripes faced the defending champions from Atlanta. Early on, the Braves played like champs, winning the first two games of the series, both played at Yankee Stadium, by a combined score of 16–1. Then the Yankee bats came alive, and they won the next two games at Atlanta-Fulton County Stadium, 5–2 and 8–6.

The pivotal game of the series pitted Andy Pettitte against John Smoltz in Game 5. Both pitchers were nearly unhittable. The Yankees managed a run in the fourth inning, and Pettitte and Wetteland made it stand up for a 1–0 victory.

New York closed out the series at home with a 3–2 win in Game 6. Mariano pitched the seventh and eighth innings. Wetteland pitched the ninth inning and earned the save—his seventh of the 1996 postseason—and was voted the World Series Most Valuable Player.

Even with Wetteland's MVP award and Pettitte's twenty-three victories on the year, everybody knew the season belonged to Mariano. He finished with an 8–3 record, posted five saves, and led the team with a stunningly low 2.09 earned run average.

Sports writers began calling him "Super Mariano." He finished third in balloting for the American League Cy Young Award, which goes to the best pitcher in each league. No setup man had ever finished that high. He was even twelfth in MVP balloting.

But none of these individual accolades meant anything to Mariano. From the beginning of his career, team success outweighed personal recognition. He cherished every moment of being a World Series champion. He loved being with his teammates as they rode down Broadway in Manhattan for a ticker tape parade. Then he flew home to Panama, where he was greeted by hundreds of fans.

"When I think of 1996, I think of Mariano Rivera," Yankee catcher and future manager Joe Girardi said.

The Yankees certainly felt the same way. During the offseason, they let the high-priced Wetteland go to the Texas Rangers and moved Mariano to closer. Wetteland was making $4 million in 1996 and wanted more. Mariano earned just $131,000. The decision seemed like a no-brainer . . . except to Mariano.

"To me, that was a crazy move," Mariano says. "When I found out that they didn't sign Wetteland, my first question was, 'Well, okay, who is going to close?'"

New York bumped up Mariano's salary to $550,000 and put him in the most pressure-packed role in baseball. At first, it appeared as if the decision would be a bust, as Mariano blew four of his first six save opportunities in 1997.

The slow start resulted in a meeting with Torre and Yankees pitching coach Mel Stottlemyre. Mariano felt terrible. He hated letting down the team.

"The harder I tried, the tougher it got," Mariano says. "It was like moving in quicksand. I kept sinking. Joe told me that 'as long as you are here, you'll be the closer.' That's exactly what I needed to hear."

Mariano rebounded to record 43 saves for the year as the Yankees finished with a 96–66 record and earned the American League wild card spot.

Mariano's first year in New York had ended with a ticker tape parade. Would every year be the same? He was about to find out.

Mariano Rivera recorded the final out in the original Yankee Stadium in 2008. Then he took some time to collect a container full of dirt from the pitcher's mound. (AP Photo/Ed Betz)

10
PARTY LIKE IT'S 1999

The Yankees have never been satisfied just to make it to the play-offs. You won't hear anybody in pinstripes saying, "I'm just happy to be here." If they advance to the postseason, they expect to win it all. That was the case in 1997, when New York met Cleveland in the American League Divisional Series.

New York won two of the first three games and stood on the brink of eliminating the Indians in Game 4. The Yankees held a 2–1 lead going into the eighth inning with Mariano coming into the game. That meant only one thing: game over.

Usually that was the case, but not on this crisp October 4 night in Cleveland. After recording the first two outs, Mariano gave up a game-tying home run to Indians catcher Sandy Alomar Jr. Cleveland went on to score a run in the bottom of the ninth inning and win 3–2. The next night, the Indians beat the Yankees 4–3 and moved on to the American League Championship Series.

In just twenty-four hours, the Yankees went from four outs away from the World Series to having their season ended. Mariano had only recently developed his miracle pitch, but it was no miracle finish for the Yankees.

The defeat would have crushed many pitchers, but Mariano stayed composed and strong. He hated to lose, but he knew he'd brought his best pitch. Alomar had just made a better swing.

Yankees Hall of Fame catcher Yogi Berra once said, "Ninety percent of this game is half mental." That statement, as odd as it sounds, may be true. But one thing is definitely true: Mariano Rivera possesses amazing mental toughness. Derek Jeter called him the most mentally tough player he's ever played with.

"I never will," Mariano says when asked why he doesn't throw his hat or get angry after a blown save. "You can't let them get to you. You have to be the same, no matter what."

The Yankees looked pretty much the same when they showed up for spring training in 1998. But early on, it was apparent that something was different. This team was more focused, more determined, and more committed to winning.

New York tore through the regular season, claiming a franchise record 114 wins. The Boston Red Sox finished in second place—22 games back—in the American League East. Those 114 wins stood as an American League record until Seattle won 116 games in 2001.

Amazingly, the Yankees were even more impressive in the playoffs. They swept Texas 3–0 in the first round then avenged the previous year's defeat by beating Cleveland four games to two in the American League Championship Series. In the World

Series, they swept the San Diego Padres in four games. Through thirteen playoff games in 1998, New York nearly doubled its opponents' run production, outscoring its foes 62–34.

Mariano did his job in the postseason. He was six for six in save opportunities and didn't give up a run. He saved three of the four World Series games, even notching a pair of two-inning saves. When he recorded the final out in New York's series-clinching 3–0 victory, he fell to the mound with his arms in the air.

"I was thanking God for everything," he says of that moment.

As good as Mariano was in 1998, he was even better in 1999. For the entire season, Mariano recorded more saves (45) than he allowed hits (43). Take away one bad streak at the beginning of July, when he blew three saves in five attempts, and Mariano may have posted the best season ever by a relief pitcher.

At the tail end of his sluggish streak, Mariano found himself on the mound in Yankee Stadium facing the Atlanta Braves. Normally, once Mariano dug his cleats into the dirt next to the pitcher's rubber, he heard nothing and could only see the catcher's mitt. But on July 16, 1999, he heard something. It was a joyous sound that he'd never heard before. He's convinced it was the voice of God.

The voice told him, "I am the One who has you here."

Mariano tried to stay focused on the game. But hearing God's voice isn't an everyday occurrence. It's hard to concentrate when you believe you've just received a message from the Lord. Mariano allowed the Braves to score four runs in the ninth inning and the Yankees lost 10–7.

From that point on, however, Mariano was nearly unhittable.

He converted his next 22 regular season save opportunities to help New York to a 98–64 record—tops in the AL East. Then he was a huge part of the Yankees' march through the playoffs.

New York beat Texas in three straight games, defeated Boston four games to one in the American League Championship series, and blasted the Braves four consecutive times in the World Series. Mariano pitched twelve-plus scoreless innings in the postseason and notched six saves.

The Yankees had won their twenty-fifth World Series title, and Mariano was voted the series' Most Valuable Player. He saved Game 1 by recording the last four outs. In Game 3, he walked away as the winning pitcher as the Yankees came from behind to win 6–5 in ten innings. And he again notched the last out to clinch the world championship in Game 4.

When asked what it felt like to be the MVP, he deflected the praise to his team.

"We all were MVPs," Mariano said. "The whole thing: manager, coaches, the twenty-five guys that were on the field."

Joe Girardi believed the honor was well deserved. "He's the best," the Yankee catcher said. "He's the best closer I've ever seen."

The Yankees had won back-to-back titles by sweeping their opponents in two straight World Series. No team had accomplished that feat since the Yankees did it in 1938 and 1939. The 1998 Yankees were called one of the best teams in baseball history, but the 1999 team was even more dominant in the postseason. Could the Yankees make it a three-peat? Their fans couldn't wait to find out.

Mariano Rivera stands strong as a baseball hero for kids in both the United States and his native Panama. He's a role model for his play on the field--and for his faith in Jesus Christ. (AP Photo/Francis Specker)

Panamanian Hero

A week after Mariano Rivera stood on his own personal float during the 1999 victory parade in New York City, he was standing next to the Panamanian president in Panama City.

During the off-season, Mariano often returned to Panama with his family. His children played with their cousins, and everybody enjoyed some rest and relaxation. But on November 3, 1999, Mariano wasn't relaxing. All eyes were on him as President Mireya Moscoso gave Mariano the Manuel Amador Guerrero Order, one of the country's highest honors.

The award was named after Panama's first president and is given to people who distinguish themselves in the arts, sciences, or politics.

Mariano spent some extra time in Panama City to speak at a church about the July night when God spoke to him. Tears rolled down his face as he described the unforgettable experience of hearing the words, "I am the One who has you here." Just like when God spoke to Moses or Paul, hearing God's voice changes a person . . . and it changed Mariano.

"That meant that the only reason I'm here is because He's my strength," Mariano said to Jack Curry of the *New York Times*. "He put me here. Without Him, I'm nothing. I think it means that He has other plans for me, to deliver His Word."

Quitting baseball wasn't out of the question. If God called him to preach, Mariano was ready to walk away. At the time, he thought he'd play four more years.

"Inside of me, I'm thinking four more years," Mariano said. "That will be enough. I love the game, but I love God more."

11
GREAT WINS AND DEVASTATING LOSSES

Repeating as World Series champion is incredibly difficult, so difficult that only ten teams in the history of baseball have achieved the feat. (Baseball historians will correctly cite that three teams prior to the 2000 season won three or more in a row. But ten teams won two straight before failing to repeat the following season.)

The Chicago Cubs accomplished the World Series repeat first, during the 1907 and '08 seasons. Then five other teams won back-to-back titles by 1930. The Philadelphia Athletics (now the Oakland A's) did it twice. The Boston Red Sox, New York Yankees, and New York Giants (the team moved to San Francisco before the 1958 season) all did it once.

After 1930, only four teams repeated as champs. The Yankees won titles in 1961 and '62 and again in 1977 and '78. The Cincinnati Reds also won two straight, in 1975 and '76. Then the Pittsburgh Pirates went back-to-back, in 1979 and '80. The World Series crown left the United States for a couple of years in 1992 and '93, when the Toronto Blue Jays were baseball's best.

Obviously, if repeating as World Series champions is extremely difficult, then achieving the "three-peat" is far more so. The Oakland A's did it in the early 1970s. And two Yankee teams did one better: from 1936 to 1939, they won four straight World Series. Then during the late 1940s and early '50s, the Bronx Bombers brought home *five* consecutive titles.

If any team was prepared to attempt the rare three-peat, it was the 2000 Yankees. Led by starting pitchers Andy Pettitte and Roger Clemens and a batting order that featured Bernie Williams, Paul O'Neill, Derek Jeter, Tino Martinez, and Jorge Posada, the Yankees had an aura of greatness.

But when you're the best, every team you play will bring its best effort to beat you. New York finished the regular season 87–74, which was good enough to win the AL East. But the team limped into the playoffs after losing fifteen of its final eighteen regular season games.

The playoffs weren't any easier as the Oakland A's pushed the Yankees to a deciding fifth game in the AL Divisional Series. Six first-inning runs and Mariano's pitching in the eighth and ninth innings made the difference as New York advanced to face Seattle in the League Championship Series.

The Mariners blanked the Yankees in the first game of the ALCS. But then Orlando Hernandez, Pettitte, and Clemens won three straight games by a combined score of 20–3 as the Yankees took a 3–1 series lead. The Yankees secured the American League championship and another trip to the World Series with a 9–7 Game 6 win at Yankee Stadium.

New York baseball fans couldn't have been happier with the World Series matchup between the Yankees and the Mets. Many people called it the "Subway Series" because fans could ride the subway to Yankee Stadium in the Bronx or to Shea Stadium (the Mets' home field) in Queens.

The Subway Series received a lot of hype, but in the end it was mostly no contest. Although every game was decided by two runs or less, the Yankees dispatched the Mets in five games. Mariano earned saves in the final two games, including an exciting Game 5 at Shea Stadium.

The two teams entered the ninth inning tied 2–2. After two straight strikeouts, the Yankees put together a two-out rally to score two runs as Posada and Scott Brosius came home. Leading 4–2, Mariano entered the game and recorded a strikeout and a walk against the first two batters he faced. With the tying run at the plate and Mets fans going crazy, Mariano calmly got Edgardo Alfonzo and Mike Piazza to hit fly balls to end the game.

New York had its three-peat!

As Yankee teammates mobbed Mariano on the mound, it marked the first time in history that the same pitcher had nailed down the final out in three consecutive World Series.

Mariano Rivera shows his competitive nature every time he steps on the mound. (AP Photo/Al Behrman)

PLAYING WITH PURPOSE: MARIANO RIVERA

Three-Peat Treat

In 1988, Los Angeles Lakers basketball coach Pat Riley submitted a trademark application for the term *three-peat*. His Lakers had just won back-to-back NBA titles and looked poised for a run at a third. Shooting guard Byron Scott came up with the term. Riley liked it so much that he applied for the trademark so he would make money every time somebody put the word on a T-shirt, hat, or coffee mug.

But Riley had to wait to earn any money on his idea. The Detroit Pistons swept the Lakers in the NBA Finals that season. Four years later, Michael Jordan's Chicago Bulls wrapped up their third straight championship, and the term *three-peat* boomed in popularity. It even made it into *Webster's Dictionary* in 2002.

Following the victory, the *New York Times* writer Jack Curry wrote, "The most crucial factor and the greatest reason the Yankees are three-time champions is Rivera. He is the infallible weapon that no other teams have."

Longtime Yankees owner George Steinbrenner gushed, "The core group, winning four World Series out of five years, in this day and age, when you have to come through layer after layer of postseason play, we can put our record, our dedication, our resolve against any team that has ever played the game of baseball."

At first glance, it would appear that the stoic and composed Panamanian and the iconic and sometimes erratic Yankee owner would have little in common. But over the years, Mariano and Steinbrenner developed a deep respect and friendship. Mariano always referred to him as "Mr. George."

When Steinbrenner died in July 2010, it hit the organization and Mariano hard.

"Mr. George, I learned a lot from that man," Mariano says. "That man always was giving, and he didn't want anyone to know. That was the most important thing to me—that he didn't want anyone to know. That man, to me . . . was one of the best."

The Yankees were certainly the best as they headed into the 2001 season. Led by strong pitching, New York won its fourth-straight AL East title with a 95–65 record. Roger Clemens won twenty games, including an American League record-tying sixteen in a row. And Mariano had his best season to date, recording 50 saves.

After dispatching Oakland and Seattle in the first two rounds of the playoffs, the Yankees found themselves on the cusp of winning a fourth-straight World Series. New York held a 2–1 lead and Mariano had the ball in the eighth inning of a deciding Game 7 against Arizona.

The eighth inning followed a typical pattern when Mariano pitches. Four batters, three strikeouts.

But in the ninth, Arizona's Mark Grace started things off with a single. The Diamondbacks, looking for the potential tying run, then attempted to bunt pinch runner David Dellucci to second. Mariano leaped from the mound, fielded the ball, and tried to throw out the lead runner at second. The ball, however, sailed into center field at Bank One Ballpark. During seven seasons in New York, Mariano had committed just one error. Now he had his second.

The next batter also bunted. This time Mariano had plenty of time to get the out at third base. That brought the Diamondbacks' leadoff hitter, Tony Womack, to the plate. Womack broke his bat hitting the ball but got enough wood on it to double down the right field line. The game was tied 2–2.

After Mariano hit Craig Counsell with a pitch, the bases were loaded for Luis Gonzalez. Gonzalez had put up career numbers in 2001, hitting 57 homers and driving in 142 runs. Yankee manager Joe Torre had a decision: play his infielders at double play depth or bring them in to try for a play at home. Torre chose to pull them in, and on the second pitch, Gonzalez hit a broken-bat flare that landed just beyond Derek Jeter's reach. Had Jeter been in his normal position, it would have been a routine out.

That didn't matter now, because Arizona had upset the Yankee dynasty to win its first World Series.

Mariano faced reporters after the game and politely answered questions. He said he had done his best and gave it everything he had.

Weeks after the disappointing loss, Mariano saw God's hand at work. Had the Yankees won the game, a ticker tape parade for the whole team would have been held back in New York City. Without a championship, Yankees teammate Enrique Wilson changed his plane flight and went home to the Dominican Republic early. Wilson had originally booked a November 12 flight on American Airlines Flight 587. Tragically, that plane crashed in Queens, New York, killing all 260 passengers on board.

"I'm glad we lost the World Series," Mariano said after discovering how that loss saved his teammate, "because it means that I still have a friend."

More difficult losses followed. New York bowed out of the 2002 playoffs in an opening-round loss to the eventual World Series champion Anaheim Angels. Then, in 2003, the Florida Marlins defeated the Yankees in the World Series by a count of four games to two.

But Mariano's greatest loss came off the field. He has often said his most treasured moments were those he spent with family and friends from church. He's just as at home in his native Panama—maybe even more so—as he is in New York or at his winter home in Tampa. In 1999, he built a two-story villa with a pool and basketball court near his childhood home in Puerto Caimito. Because he plays baseball most of the time, he hired family members to care for his place year-round.

After the Yankees defeated Minnesota in the 2004 AL Divisional Series, Mariano received unthinkable news: two of his cousins had died in his swimming pool in Panama. Victor Darío Avila, his wife's first cousin and a childhood friend of Mariano's, worked at the home as a gardener. His teenaged son, Victor, often joined his dad to help out. The two were found electrocuted in the water after a live electrical cable ended up in the pool.

Mariano and Clara immediately flew to Panama to comfort family members and help with funeral arrangements. The l... devastated everybody in the tightly knit fishing vil... did everything he could for his family, attended... then boarded a private plane back to New York.

Over the years Mariano Rivera and shortstop Derek Jeter (right) have been part of five World Series championship teams for the New York ... es. During that time, ... developed a deep ... for each other. ... (Nam Y. Huh)

he landed at the airport and went straight to the stadium.

Showing tremendous focus and resolve, he saved Game 1 against the Boston Red Sox. He doesn't remember eating or sleeping before the game, but he got the job done on the field.

"The most difficult part of my day was leaving my family, knowing they are still in pain," Mariano said. "It was tough coming on that plane alone. There's tears coming out of my eyes . . . but I have a job to do, and I have twenty-four players there waiting for me."

He notched a save in Game 2 as well. In fact, the Yankees led the series 3–0 before Boston rolled off four straight victories to end New York's season.

With the season ended, Mariano could get back to his family. He usually spent a month around Christmas in Panama. But this year, the memories of the loss of his cousins were too fresh and too painful. Instead of traveling down to Panama, he flew thirty family members to the United States. He spent the winter lifting weights and riding his stationary bike at home. He didn't throw a ball until spring training because he felt he needed to be away from baseball and with his family instead.

Throughout Mariano's career, his priorities have been clear: faith, family, baseball. That consistency of character has earned him the respect of teammates and opponents alike.

12
SPEAK THE TRUTH

On the mound, Mariano Rivera always looks the same. His throwing motion is the same. His expression is the same. And the results are usually the same—a Yankee victory.

He never smiles, except maybe after the game is over and he's closed out a playoff victory or World Series title. He doesn't gloat after strikeouts and doesn't stare down batters. He's serious about doing his job and doing it well.

Off the mound, Mariano's true personality shows itself.

"He's always got a smile on his face, and people don't see that," longtime Yankee catcher Jorge Posada says. "In the clubhouse, he's completely different than the guy people see on the mound. He's a great friend and a great person."

Talk to other Yankee players, and you'll hear the same thing. It doesn't matter if they've worn the pinstripes for one season or for a decade: they all admire Mariano.

"He's like my brother," says Derek Jeter, who came up in the minor leagues with Mo. "Any time you play with someone that long, there's a connection there. . . . He's been the exact same person he was since the first day I met him."

Outfielder Johnny Damon, who played for the Yankees from 2006 to 2009, says one of the reasons he wanted to put on the pinstripes was so he wouldn't have to face Mariano as an opposing batter. Mike Mussina, who pitched for the Yankees from 2001 to 2008, was once asked about his favorite part of pitching in New York. Mussina didn't hesitate: "Mariano was my answer. To know that he's out there in the bullpen, it's comforting to know you have somebody who is going to handle those last outs."

Mariano's consistency comes largely from his faith in Jesus Christ. Over and over again, the Yankee closer has credited God for helping make him the player he is on the mound and the person he is off of it.

"I cannot move without His direction," Mariano says. "That doesn't mean that I'm a perfect man. Now I wish I could tell you that I'm perfect, but I'm not. But I'm always trying to please the Lord, and that's my goal."

Since joining the Yankees, he's been a fixture at team Bible studies. He can often be found reading his Bible in the clubhouse before and after games. During his time away from the ballpark, Mariano preaches at churches—in both Spanish and English—and shares about his faith in Christ at other community events. He deeply desires for people to know God and to live good lives.

That concern for other people is genuine. Bernie Williams,

who had a locker near Mariano's for years in the Yankee clubhouse, said, "Mo reaches out to everybody; he's a great teammate and motivator, especially to young guys. He likes to take them under his wing, share his faith with them, and take care of them."

When Mariano reads Proverbs 27:17—"As iron sharpens iron, so a friend sharpens a friend" (NLT)—he doesn't see just words. He sees a calling for his Yankee teammates to keep each other accountable and encourage each other to be better players and better people.

Rookie Relief

Mariano Rivera knows how difficult it is for young players to navigate their way through the minor leagues. He had to overcome a language barrier and learn a new culture and a new position. Without the help of key people, he may never have found his way to a personal relationship with God and made his way to the Yankees.

Mariano wants to be that key person for future players. He has a heart for rookies, especially for young players from Latin America. He often approaches them at spring training to encourage them to learn English and to stay away from destructive behaviors such as getting drunk, staying out late, and doing drugs.

"It's a hard road in the minor leagues," Mariano says. "During the process from the minor leagues to the big leagues, there are a lot of things that can take you to other ways that are not the way that you came to do it. Therefore, I'd like to work with the guys to make sure they understand why they came here and what their goals and their rules are."

Mariano Rivera's actions have earned him the admiration of teammates, opponents, and managers. Here former Yankees skipper Joe Torre congratulates Mariano after his 300th career save. (AP Photo/Steve Nesius)

Mariano is deeply committed to his teammates. He bleeds Yankee blue and often tells reporters that he'd never want to pitch for another team. The closer is also the first to say that he never could have collected so many saves if his team hadn't put him in the right situation. And once that situation arises, Mariano always appears tranquil on the mound—and it's a peace that comes from knowing the Prince of Peace.

"I don't know if we'll ever see it again," Yankee manager Joe Girardi said after Mariano notched his 600th career save. "This is a guy who I believe is the best closer that's ever been in the game, and I've had the fortune of catching him, coaching him, and managing him, and it's a treat."

Posada agrees: "You're seeing the greatest closer of all time. I don't care about eras. There's nobody better. No one can even compare. His body doesn't change. He doesn't change. He's the same Mariano as he was as a setup man, as a closer, and as a friend."

Mariano was shy when he first stepped into the Yankee clubhouse as a starting pitcher. It took other players a little while to get to know him. Now everybody knows who he is. He's a jokester who isn't shy about ribbing his friends, and he enjoys baseball banter and can take it as well as he can give it. But he's also a standup guy who sets the tone in the clubhouse.

"He's better than any guy I have ever seen," Jeter says. "The most amazing thing is Mo's demeanor; not too many people have what he has. He's never intimidated; he'll challenge anyone. And you can't tell from his expression whether he was successful the night before or if he failed the night before."

Mariano doesn't just challenge opposing batters—he challenges his own teammates. He first sets a tone by the way he prepares, approaches, and plays the game. But he also challenges them with his words. He doesn't say things in an unkind way. Just like the Bible teaches, he speaks the truth in love. He'll tell the hard truth, but his teammates know he does it because he loves them.

Several months after Curtis Granderson joined the Yankees in 2010, Mariano jogged over for a talk as the two shagged balls in the outfield during batting practice. Granderson had struggled since coming to New York, hitting under .250. Mariano knew the center fielder was key to the team's success heading into the playoffs and in future years.

"He was telling me about things he wanted me to do to help the team," Granderson says about the encounter. "General stuff about how I could help the team, things I needed to do to help the lineup, things I needed to improve on. I was really appreciative that he would take the time. When Mariano talks, you listen."

No player is off-limits, not even the highest paid player in baseball, Alex Rodriguez. During a stretch in 2011, A-Rod was searching for his swing and Mariano wanted to help him find it. He took Rodriguez into the training room for a private conversation. It wasn't the first time.

"He'll call me into the trainer's room and say, 'What are you doing?' . . . or 'You're not right; we've got to get you right.' Stuff like that," Rodriguez says. "It's so refreshing. You wouldn't expect that from Mariano Rivera, getting in my face. . . . But he's like my brother, one of my best friends. It's awesome. It's priceless."

As a friend and team leader, Mariano has made a huge impact on the Yankees.

"Equally as impressive as 600 [saves], is what he's done in here for everyone as a leader," Rodriguez says. "Whatever he's done on the field, or however tough he is to face, what a great leader he's been to me and what a great teammate and friend."

Mariano says he doesn't have any friends when he steps on the mound, but he has a lot of them in everyday life—even players on other teams. Through his integrity and consistent actions, Mariano has become one of the most respected and beloved players in baseball.

13
MORE THAN A
LITTLE RESPECT

Every great athlete should have a great nickname. Hockey super-star Wayne Gretzky is still called "The Great One." Basketball Hall of Famer Michael Jordan was known as "His Airness." LeBron James goes by "King James."

With his chiseled facial features and stoic mannerisms, Mariano Rivera looks like he belongs to baseball royalty. What he lacks, however, is a nickname worthy of his position in the sport.

Some have called him the "Hammer of God." He's also been known as "The Sandman" and "Super Mariano." But music and video game tie-ins just don't seem to work for Mariano. Then there's "The Panama Express." Too Nolan Ryan? Probably. Plus, Mariano relies more on the movement of his cut fastball than the speed of it. Ironically, the nickname that's stuck the best is the one he's had the longest. Friends and teammates simply call him "Mo."

Mariano Rivera's love of family can be seen on his face as his youngest son, Jaziel, receives a gift from New York manager Joe Girardi in a ceremony before a game at Yankee Stadium. (AP Photo/Kathy Willens)

That's not very flashy—and certainly not very royal—but maybe that's why it fits. For a player who's so often in the spotlight, Mariano prefers having the spotlight focused on his team, not on himself. He's also an extremely private man who's protective of his wife and three sons: Mariano Jr., Jafet, and Jaziel. He would much rather speak to the media about his teammates than himself. But, of course, it's the media that want Mariano to have a cool nickname.

Years ago, ESPN sportscaster Chris Berman asked the public to help create a fitting nickname for the Yankee closer. More than fifteen hundred suggestions came in. Fans then voted on their favorites, and a New Jersey resident's suggestion of "Mo Batter Blues" won. (Feel free to groan.) Other ideas included, "The Save-ior," "The Panamaniac," and "The Hudson Rivera." Obviously, none of those stuck either—or *should* have.

But what has stuck is Mariano's reputation around the league. Baseball writer Peter Gammons, who has covered the sport for more than forty years, has said the player he most respects is Mariano. Derek Jeter agrees, saying, "I think everyone who knows him feels the same way."

Opponents may respect Mariano, but they certainly don't like hitting against him. The Yankees and the Boston Red Sox have one of the most heated rivalries in sports, but Red Sox great David Ortiz doesn't mind praising Mariano. "If you talk to him at an All-Star Game, it's like talking to somebody who just got called up," Ortiz said. "To him, everybody else is good. I don't get it. To him, everybody else is the best. It's unbelievable. And he is the greatest. . . . Good people, you want to do well."

Mariano is "good people." His parents brought him up with traditional values. They taught him to respect everybody, to treat everybody like family.

"I don't wait for people to give me respect," Mariano says. "I always give them respect. Any player. Even a rookie, an old player, a veteran. I never try to show up anybody. I go to my business. I always take time for somebody who wants to talk to me. That's my thing."

Respect for No. 42

Mariano Rivera is the last big league player to wear No. 42 on his everyday uniform. It's an honor he doesn't take lightly.

In 1997, Major League Baseball retired the number to honor Jackie Robinson, the first man to break baseball's color barrier. Before April 15, 1947, African American players couldn't compete in the major leagues. But Robinson broke through that wall of segregation when he laced up his cleats for the Brooklyn Dodgers. He faced threats, taunts, and physical attacks on the field. He endured it all and ultimately changed the face of professional baseball.

About a dozen players were allowed to keep wearing No. 42 when baseball made the decision to retire Robinson's number. Mariano was given the number as a twenty-five-year-old rookie. Before making it to the big leagues, he wore No. 58.

"Being the only one carrying the number right now, and forever, this means a lot to me," Mariano says.

In January 2010, Mariano met Rachel Robinson, Jackie's

widow, for the first time. Mariano said it was an honor to meet her, and she shared the same sentiment.

"I've been very pleased that he is the last one to wear Jack's number," Rachel Robinson said. "I had admired Mariano Rivera for so long from afar."

His thing is also winning—and that also garners a lot of respect around the majors.

David Justice played for the Atlanta Braves for eight years in the early 1990s before moving to Cleveland and eventually playing on the Yankees' 2000 World Series championship team. It didn't take him long to figure out Mariano's worth to his club.

"If we had Rivera in Atlanta, we would have won about three or four World Series," said Justice, who won one title with the Braves, in 1995. "He's that good. I'm telling you, he's every bit of what they say about him and then some."

The "then some" includes Mariano's intangibles—the traits that can't be described with words or measured by statistics but help lift a team to victory. Many baseball experts have said that the Panama Express's (see, the nickname just doesn't do him justice) presence raises everybody's confidence. The Yankees know that if they play seven or eight strong innings, Mariano can finish the deal.

"To have a guy like him is a tremendous psychological advantage," former Yankee closer Rich "Goose" Gossage said. "There's a feeling of invincibility and being bullet-proof. Rivera has that going for him."

More than anything, though, Mariano has kindness and years of goodwill going for him. Ever since he entered the league—and even before that—he has lived by the Golden Rule. "I believe that one will never go wrong treating people the way you want them to treat you," he says.

Mariano has always been generous in trying to help others. He's shown generosity with how he spends his time . . . and how he uses his money.

New York Yankees first baseman Tino Martinez (No. 24) jumps into the arms of pitcher Mariano Rivera as other teammates also celebrate the Yankees' third straight World Series title in 2000. (AP Photo/Bill Kostroun)

14
FIRM FOUNDATION

Mariano may have grown up near the beach in Puerto Caimito, but he certainly hasn't built his life on the sand.

In the Bible, Jesus tells the story of two builders—a wise one and a foolish one. The wise man built his house on a foundation of rock, but the foolish builder constructed his home on sand. When the rains came, the winds blew, and the streams rose, the house on the rock stood strong. The house on the sand, however, came crashing down.

Mariano has a firm foundation. His life is built on *the* Rock, Jesus Christ. He studies God's Word and puts its principles into practice, and he tries to honor God with his actions, including how he uses his enormous wealth.

It's no secret that baseball players make a lot of money.

Mariano's teammate Alex Rodriguez makes more than $30 million a year playing baseball. While Mariano started out earning

$550,000 during his first season as a closer in 1997, two years later he was making $4.2 million. Between 2003 and 2012, his yearly salary ranged between $10 million and $15 million.

Mariano and Clara wanted to share the blessings God had given their family with others, so in 1998, they set up the Mariano Rivera Foundation. The foundation is mainly focused on children's education, health, and wellness. Every year, Mariano's foundation donates more than $500,000 to underprivileged families in the United States and Panama.

"The foundation started like this," Mariano says. "We were making good money. Whatever I made was tithed to a church I was a member of—10 percent of my salary. I was giving a lot of money, so I decided to put this into a fund so we could help many churches and many people in need."

For years, Mariano would travel back to Panama with his family for Christmas. Not only would he bring presents for his parents, aunts, uncles, cousins, nieces, and nephews, but he'd bring a couple of container loads of gifts for needy kids. He'd go around the country—into the mountains and to small villages—to hand out the toys.

"You go into villages where they don't have anything," Mariano says. "And the smile these kids have on their faces is priceless. I know it's not going to solve the problem, but it's something. And it brings joy." Mariano knows that a little joy can go a long way. And he has a connection with the kids he tries to help.

While the call to help the needy comes from the rock-solid foundation of the Bible, Mariano's desire to give actually has sandy beginnings. He still remembers how policemen would drive around

Puerto Caimito and hand out toys to him and other children. He was seven or eight when a policeman gave him a little toy train.

Giving to the True Closers

Following the September 11, 2001, terrorist attacks in New York City and Washington, DC, the major leagues suspended competition for six days. When games resumed, it proved that the terrorists wouldn't win. Americans would continue to gather in large groups to cheer on their teams.

The events of 9/11 deeply affected Mariano and his teammates. They spent a lot of time that fall visiting hospitals and fire stations and doing anything they could to lift people's spirits. After the season ended, Mariano did even more.

That year, he set a then-personal best of 50 saves and earned the American League Rolaids Relief Man Award. At the awards ceremony, the fireman's hat-shaped trophy stayed in Mariano's hands for only moments before he gave it to New York City fire commissioner Thomas Von Essen.

"I want to present this trophy to the true saviors, the true closers," Mariano said.

As Mariano puts it, "I remember what the firefighters did in 2001. I'm saving games; they're saving lives. They're putting their lives on the line to save other people."

The Yankee closer doesn't bring just toys to give away in his home country. He's also purchased baseball equipment for local children, donated medical equipment and supplies to a hospital, and funded two computer labs in Panama. Statistics show that six out of ten people in the United States own computers. In many Latin American countries, however, only one out of a thousand people has a computer. But computer skills are important to finding a job and getting ahead in life. Mariano understands that, and that's why he funded the computer labs.

Mariano's foundation also provides scholarships for children who show aptitude in certain subjects. And it's not for just the A-plus students; Mariano also looks for those B students who show tremendous talent but who haven't had an opportunity to show it.

"Scholarships give opportunities to kids and families who don't have much," Mariano says. "They can become somebody, a graduate, a doctor. But they can't do it alone."

Mariano doesn't just focus on the children; he helps parents as well. He honored mothers in Puerto Caimito by holding a party on Mother's Day (which is celebrated on December 8 in Panama) and giving away furniture and appliances. He even built a church in his hometown where families can worship God.

No. 42 also stays involved with a number of charities in the United States. Mariano and his wife have become involved with The Guidance Center, an organization that has helped needy people in New Rochelle and Westchester County (an area northeast of New York City) for more than seventy years. It's not unusual for the Riveras to spend some of their holidays helping the less fortunate. In 2011, Mariano, Clara, and others helped give away bags filled with food—turkey, beans, rice, vegetables, potatoes, and canned goods—at Thanksgiving.

"In the foundation, we try to spread out our efforts as much as we can," Mariano says. "I like to include my wife, my kids, and everybody who wants to help."

Mariano's charity work hasn't gone unnoticed. In 2003, he

Though most of his life is lived in the public eye, Mariano Rivera likes to keep much of his extensive charity work private. (AP Photo/Julie Jacobson)

was honored with the Thurman Munson Award—named for the great Yankee catcher who died in 1979—which recognizes excellence on the field and in the community. He's even been mentioned in the "Giving Back 30," an annual list of thirty celebrities who give the most to charity.

Mariano neither wants nor seeks the accolades. He'd prefer to do his giving in private. Much of what his foundation accomplishes is done discreetly and without fanfare. His heart's desire is to follow what Jesus said about giving in Matthew 6:2: "When you give to someone in need, don't do as the hypocrites do—blowing trumpets in the synagogues and streets to call attention to their acts of charity! I tell you the truth, they have received all the reward they will ever get" (NLT).

Mariano has plenty of earthly treasures, but he's laying up treasures in heaven as well. He believes giving is between himself, his family, and God. Like longtime Yankee owner George Steinbrenner, Mariano doesn't want to draw attention to himself with his giving. People who knew Steinbrenner reported that the Yankee owner would say that if more than two people knew about an act of kindness between one person and another—then it was one too many.

Steinbrenner and Mariano shared another passion besides helping others: winning. Steinbrenner once said, "Winning is the most important thing in my life, after breathing. Breathing first, winning next." The Yankees did plenty of winning during Steinbrenner's thirty-eight years as the club's principal owner. But after winning their third World Series in a row in 2000, it took awhile before they got back on top.

15
BACK ON TOP

Sports fans love to talk about the best teams ever. Sometimes a team will put together one magical season where it can't be beat. Even more impressive, though, are the teams that win year after year.

In the National Basketball Association, the Boston Celtics and Los Angeles Lakers have consistently been at or near the top ever since the league formed in 1947. As of the end of the 2011–12 season, the Celtics and Lakers (who originally played in Minnesota—the Land of 10,000 Lakes) had combined to win *half* of the NBA championships. Boston had claimed seventeen titles, the Lakers sixteen.

In hockey, no team can compare to the Montreal Canadiens. As of the end of the 2011–12 season, the Canadiens had played in the Stanley Cup Finals thirty-four times and taken home the championship trophy on twenty-four occasions.

Figuring out who is the all-time best in professional football is a little more difficult. Although the National Football League held its first official league championship game in 1933 (championships were determined by won-lost records before that), the first Super Bowl wasn't played until the 1966–67 season. As of the end of the 2011–12 season, the Pittsburgh Steelers had the most Super Bowl wins with six. But if all NFL championships are taken into account (Super Bowls *and* NFL championships), then Green Bay is clearly the best. In addition to winning four Super Bowls, the Packers have won nine NFL championships.

In baseball, no franchise can compare with the New York Yankees. Their World Series title in 2000 was their twenty-sixth championship (at the conclusion of the 2012 season, St. Louis was a distant second on the list with eleven). But it would be nine years before they won their twenty-seventh.

The 2008 Yankees finished third in the American League East with an 89–73 record and missed the playoffs for the first time since 1993. The disappointment of the season led New York to retool its roster heading into 2009. During the off-season, the Yankees addressed their greatest need: starting pitching and power hitting. When the Yankees signed pitchers CC Sabathia and A.J. Burnett and hard-hitting first baseman Mark Teixeira, they showed they were serious about contending for another World Series title.

As the Yankees took the field in 2009, they had a new look and a renewed determination to get back on top. But it wasn't just the roster that looked new at the beginning of the season—New York was also playing in a brand-new Yankee Stadium.

Closing Act

In 1923, Babe Ruth hit the first-ever home run in Yankee Stadium. On September 21, 2008, Mariano Rivera threw the last pitch. Both games ended in a New York victory. The Yankees defeated the Boston Red Sox 4-1 in the first game played at Yankee Stadium. New York beat Baltimore in the storied stadium's final game.

When Mariano entered the contest in the ninth inning of that last game, the Yankees already led 7-3. It wasn't a save situation, but manager Joe Girardi could think of no better person to end things on the mound. In typical fashion, Mariano mowed down the Orioles in 1-2-3 order. After the last out, Mariano kept the game ball and gave it to George Steinbrenner.

"Mr. George, he gave me the opportunity, and he gave me the chance," Mariano said. "The least I can do is give the ball to him."

Babe Ruth's daughter, Julia Ruth Stevens, had thrown out the ceremonial first pitch as a picture of her dad was shown on the scoreboard next to the message, TO BE CONTINUED . . .

The following spring, the new Yankee Stadium, which was constructed at a cost of $1.5 billion, was christened. The original Yankee Stadium was built for $2.5 million.

The Yankees started the season slowly. They lost their first two games, including their first-ever at the new Yankee Stadium. But once Alex Rodriguez joined the club in May (after recovering from off-season hip surgery), the team started to find its stride. New York won eight straight games after the All-Star break and

In 2009, the New York Yankees and pitcher Mariano Rivera found their stride after Alex Rodriguez rejoined the team in May after recovering from surgery. (AP Photo/Julie Jacobson)

went on to post the best record in baseball at 103–59.

Along the way, the Yankees had plenty of highlights. On September 11, Derek Jeter became the Yankees' all-time hits leader when he smacked his 2,722nd—one more than Yankee great Lou Gehrig. New York also set a team record for home runs in a season by hitting 243 bombs (the 2004 Yankees "went yard" 242 times).

Entering the playoffs, most everyone agreed that the two teams to beat were the defending world champion Philadelphia Phillies from the National League and the Yankees from the American League.

New York swept Minnesota in the opening round then beat the Los Angeles Angels in six games in the AL Championship Series.

To nobody's surprise, New York faced Philadelphia in the World Series. The Phillies took Game 1 by a 6–1 score, but three straight Yankee victories put them on the threshold of reclaiming the crown.

New York secured its twenty-seventh world championship on November 5, 2009. And who was on the mound when the Yankees recorded the decisive out in Game Six? Mariano, of course.

Mariano earned saves in Game 2 and Game 4. And although New York led 7–3 in the eighth inning of Game 6, Yankee manager Joe Girardi wanted his best man on the mound to close out the contest. Girardi had been the catcher the last time New York had won the Series. Now the second-year manager didn't want to take any chances.

Mariano notched the last five outs, including a final out that seemed to go on forever. Mo had to throw ten pitches to Shane

Victorino, who fouled off four two-strike pitches. Finally, the Phillies center fielder grounded to Robinson Cano at second base. After Cano threw the ball to Teixeira at first, Teixeira thrust his right arm in the air and took off across the diamond. All the Yankees jumped into a huge pile.

While it was the first World Series title for Teixeira, Rodriguez, Sabathia, and others, it earned Mariano, Jeter, Andy Pettitte, and Jorge Posada their fifth world championship rings.

"It's wonderful to be able to play with those bunch of guys," Mariano said after the game. "It's like working for a company with four people for your whole career. God bless those guys."

Burnett, the winning pitcher in Game 2, may have been in his first year with New York, but he'd already gained an appreciation for what Mariano, Jeter, Pettitte, and Posada meant to the franchise.

"They're guys who really showed you how to be a New York Yankee," Burnett said. "And they do that by being themselves, by showing class, and by being the most humble human beings I've ever been around."

As Jeter received the championship trophy after the game, the other members of the "Core Four" stood by his side. Pettitte, who won two games in the Series (including the clincher), said the first championship, in 1996, would always be the sweetest, but that this one was special because it took so long to get back into the winner's circle.

Mariano agreed: "I never forgot, but when you're in there you know how much you missed it. You find out, definitely, how moving it is to be in this position. To be the last team standing on the mound and win the whole thing, it's priceless."

The victory was also especially meaningful to Girardi, who had chosen to wear No. 27 when he took over as Yankee manager in 2008. The number symbolized his goal of bringing a twenty-seventh World Series title to New York. Following a disappointing first season as Yankee skipper, Girardi faced a lot of pressure to win in 2009. The victory took that pressure off his back.

Reclaiming the championship also helped ease the pain of one of Mariano's lowest moments on the mound. The win over the Phillies came on the eighth anniversary of the night Mariano lost Game 7 of the 2001 World Series to Arizona. He had claimed his Major League record ninth and tenth saves in the World Series against Philadelphia.

But less than two years later, Mariano would make an even bigger save.

16
THE CHURCH RIVERA SAVED

Before Yankee Stadium was known as "The Home of Champions," it was called the "House That Ruth Built" because of the exploits of George Herman Ruth. You might know him better as "Babe."

Early in the twentieth century, Babe Ruth was the biggest thing in baseball. After he led the Boston Red Sox to three World Series championships, the Yankees purchased Babe's contract on January 5, 1920, for $125,000. New York baseball fans flocked to see the "Sultan of Swat." That season, the Yankees drew more fans to the Polo Grounds in Manhattan than baseball's New York Giants. (Just like the National Football League's New York Jets and Giants now share a stadium, baseball's Yankees and Giants shared the Polo Grounds from 1913–22.)

In 1921, the Yankees announced a purchase of ten acres in the Bronx. They had decided to build their own ballpark that

Saving a church gives Mariano Rivera as much reason to celebrate as saving a game for his Yankees. (AP Photo/ Elise Amendola)

favored left-handed power hitters, with a right field fence only 295 feet from home plate. Ruth was the game's best left-handed hitter—and by the time he finished his career, he had walloped what was then a major league record 714 home runs.

When Yankee Stadium opened in 1923, New York christened it in grand fashion by winning that season's World Series. Experts agreed that without Babe's star power, the Yankees may not have been able to build their iconic home. It immediately became known as the "House That Ruth Built."

In all, Yankee Stadium hosted 33 World Series, with the home team winning 26 championships. The stadium hosted its final game in 2008

Nearly three years after the House that Ruth Built shut its doors, Mariano vowed to help reopen the doors of North Avenue Church in New Rochelle, New York. The beautiful stone building had once been home to the largest Presbyterian church in Westchester County. Built in 1907, North Avenue Church played a significant role in New Rochelle's history. But more recently, it sat unoccupied. The city had owned it for decades, and it had fallen into disrepair.

In June 2011, Mariano and his fellow Spanish-speaking congregants at *Refugio de Esperanza*—Refuge of Hope—announced that they wanted to buy and restore the historic building, which stands near City Hall. Initially, Mariano's church leased and slowly rebuilt the building that had become a safety risk.

"We have a lot of goals that we want to fulfill, but the main goal right now is to restore the church," Mariano said at a press conference.

Renovation costs were estimated at $3 million, but the price didn't concern the Yankee closer, who for years had lived in New Rochelle with his family. Mariano said he fell in love with the building from the moment he saw it and had big plans for the church.

Headlines immediately appeared on the Internet and in newspapers, saying ANOTHER SAVE FOR YANKEES' MARIANO RIVERA or ONE MORE SAVE FOR YANKEES' CLOSER. But in the end, this project may become known simply as "The Church That Rivera Saved."

This wasn't Mariano's first experience with church building. His foundation has helped construct churches in Panama, Mexico, and Puerto Rico.

New Rochelle mayor Noam Bramson said he was excited to see the church brought "back to its former luster, and with its original purpose, as a house of worship."

The building will serve as a house of worship on Sundays, but its doors will remain open during the week as a community center that offers education and support services for families. And, like most projects Mariano funds, the church will have an emphasis on helping children. The Yankee great said the church will host after-school programs and possibly sponsor a youth baseball team.

"We have a lot of goals to work with the youth," Mariano said. "That is my passion. We are working hard to make it open as soon as possible."

Mariano added that he plans to devote himself to the church

The Perfect Cardboard Glove

Mariano Rivera loves passing down his passion for baseball to the next generation of players. Whether it's sponsoring youth baseball teams, teaching young players how to throw his cut fastball, or providing proper equipment to the less fortunate, Mariano does all he can to see kids thrive in the sport.

The best closer in baseball history has plenty of knowledge and wise tips to share, including how to make the perfect cardboard glove. That's what Mariano used as a child, although he doesn't recommend it for young players who can afford to get a real glove.

During a video interview with sports marketer Brandon Steiner, Mariano demonstrated his glove-making abilities, using just a knife and a piece of cardboard.

"I love this glove," Mariano said as he carefully worked the blade with his nimble fingers. "It's priceless."

Mariano explained that it hurt to use his bare hand to field fly balls and grounders when he was a kid, so he and his friends created these makeshift gloves.

To watch a YouTube video of Mariano making a cardboard glove, do an Internet search for "Mariano Rivera Talks about His First Glove."

full-time once he retires from baseball. Yankees fans, of course, hope that's years down the road.

"The game is my job, but life continues," Mariano said. "Baseball will stop one day, and I will have to step up. This is what I want to do."

Mariano has often said that after baseball he'd like to become

Mariano Rivera, left, tries to pass down his love of the Yankees and what it means to play in the pinstripes to younger teammates such as Curtis Granderson. (AP Photo/Frank Franklin II)

a pastor or an evangelist. No matter what he does, he plans to give back. Mariano knows that God has blessed him with tremendous physical, material, and relational gifts. He has a beautiful family and tremendous financial resources, but he wants to do more than write checks or fix churches.

"It's not just reaching into your pocket to give back," Mariano says. "You have to give what's the most important thing—time. When you give your time, it costs."

That willingness to give his time off the field—along with his play on it—has made Mariano one of the most beloved Yankees of all time.

17
A LEGEND AMONG LEGENDS

No Major League Baseball team has more legends than the New York Yankees. It's not too much of an exaggeration to say that the retired numbers displayed at Yankee Stadium represent a Who's Who of Hall of Famers.

Babe Ruth wore No. 3 for the Yankees and hit 714 career home runs—a big league record that stood until Hank Aaron of the Atlanta Braves smacked his 715th homer on April 8, 1974. (Hammerin' Hank finished his career in 1976 with 755 homers.) Babe also won almost 100 games as a pitcher.

Many baseball experts consider Joe DiMaggio the best all-around player in history. The legendary Yankee center fielder wore No. 5 and is celebrated for saying, "I'd like to thank the good Lord for making me a Yankee." Many believe his 56-game hitting streak is a record that will never be broken.

Yankee slugger Lou Gehrig played a record-setting 2,130

games in a row at first base. The mark stood until September 6, 1995, when Cal Ripken Jr. of the Baltimore Orioles played in his 2,131st consecutive game. (Ripken extended his streak to 2,632 games before voluntarily sitting out a game in 1998.) Forced into early retirement by a terminal illness that now bears his name, Gehrig made his famous "Today, I consider myself the luckiest man on the face of the earth" speech on July 4, 1939. In 1942, No. 4's life was depicted in the famous movie *The Pride of the Yankees*.

Mickey Mantle will forever be the Yankees' No. 7. Although he retired in 1968, Mantle still holds numerous all-time World Series hitting records. Few players have ever been better in clutch situations.

Billy Martin made his name in the World Series as well. The fierce competitor with a great baseball mind wore No. 1 for the Yankees from 1950 to 1956. After retiring as a player, Martin came back to New York to manage the team for eight years during the 1970s and 80s.

Yogi Berra, who wore No. 8 for the Yankees, brought more to the game than his colorful and funny quotes. He was the third player to win three Most Valuable Player awards in a row, and his ten World Series championships are the most in baseball history. Berra also spent time as a Yankees coach and manager.

Roger Maris is best known for hitting 61 home runs during the 1961 season, which broke Babe Ruth's single-season record of 60 in 1927. Maris' mark fell in 1998. No. 9 is still known as one of the best gloves among Yankee right fielders.

The list of Yankee greats is so impressive that there's no need to look beyond the single digits. In all, the Yankees have retired fifteen different numbers, including those of pitchers Whitey Ford (No. 16) and Ron Guidry (No. 49).

But when it comes to legendary Yankees pitchers, Mariano is right at the top of the list—and that list includes legends such as Ford, Guidry, Lefty Gomez, Red Ruffing, and Rich "Goose" Gossage.

Gossage, a Hall of Famer himself, said he knew Mariano was going to be great the first time he saw No. 42 play on TV.

"He has no fear of failure," Gossage said. "The first time I saw him was on TV when the Yankees were playing Seattle in the playoffs [in 1995]. He pitches like five innings over three games, doesn't allow a run. Comes on in the eighth in Game 5. Bases loaded, tie game. Strikes out a guy on three pitches. He's intense, but very focused, very calm."

Mariano has continued to enjoy success and has been the picture of calm ever since. By the end of the 2011 season, Mo held twenty-nine major league pitching records and eight career Yankee records, including a couple he set during an incredible streak from 1998 to 2000. No Yankee pitcher has ever had a better strikeout-to-walk ratio. Over the course of his career, Mariano has struck out four batters for every one that he's walked.

Mariano's consistency and dominance are truly amazing. Sportswriters have predicted his decline for years. After several blown saves early in one season, the *Albany Times Union* published the headline, RIVERA NO LONGER MR. AUTOMATIC. That

New York Yankees Hall of Fame catcher Yogi Berra, left, poses beside Mariano Rivera with a gift from the team. One of Rivera's sons, right, also enjoyed the pregame festivities. (AP Photo/Kathy Willens)

was in 2002. Since then, he's had some of his best years and has been every bit as automatic as he was in the late '90s.

In 2004, he earned a career-high 53 saves. In 2009, he recorded 44 regular season saves, then added 5 more in the postseason to help the Yankees win the World Series.

"Let's face it," former Yankee manager Joe Torre said. "The regular season for Mo is great, but that's the cupcakes and the ice cream. What separates him from everybody else is what he's done in the postseason."

Through the 2012 season, Mariano has thrown 140 postseason innings. That's as many innings as most major league closers throw in two full *regular* seasons. During those innings, he's recorded a phenomenal 42 saves, with eight wins against a single loss.

"That comes from God, having the ability to perform," Mariano says. "I always thank God that He has given me the chance to be part of a team like the New York Yankees and to be able to do my job every time I get there."

Ultimate Closer

In 2005, Mariano Rivera sat down with *Sports Illustrated* website columnist Dave Hollander. They talked about the pitcher's faith and good fortune to have become a Yankee. Then they had this candid exchange about Jesus Christ:

Hollander: If Jesus was a major league pitcher, would He be a starter, middle reliever, or a closer?

Mariano: Man, He would be everything—starter, middle reliever, and closer. He would do it all.

Hollander: Would it be fair to say Jesus could've been the ultimate middle reliever, willing to sacrifice Himself for the poor play of others that came before Him and possessing the humility to allow the pitcher who comes after Him to get all the glory?

Mariano: He'll sacrifice for the team, for the world, and for the Holy Spirit—the one that came after Him. Jesus would be the ultimate starter, middle reliever, and closer, because if He starts it, He finishes it.

Hollander: But maybe He's a natural closer, after all, since so many people see Him as their Savior?

Mariano: That's definitely true.

Before the 2010 season started, Mariano turned forty, but age didn't appear to have slowed him down. He had 33 saves that season and helped the Yankees through the first round of the playoffs.

The following year, Mariano was even better, amassing 44 saves, including two record-breaking performances. On May 28, 2011, Mariano appeared in his 1,000th game as a Yankee. Fourteen major league pitchers before him had appeared in 1,000 games, but he was the first to do it with one team. His stats that night: four batters, three outs, and twelve pitches—ten of which were strikes.

Then, on September 19, Mariano broke the all-times saves record by notching his 602nd.

"There's no doubt," Yankee teammate Mark Teixeira said about Mariano's name being at the top of all-time greatest closers.

"He deserves to be on top of it. In sports, I can't think of a better guy to play one position. There's arguments . . . basketball: Jordan, LeBron, whoever. With this one, there's definitely not an argument."

Mariano's legacy grows every season, as more and more young pitchers try to develop a cut fastball. But he doesn't worry too much about how he's remembered on a baseball field. At the same time, the Yankee great is the kind of player who doesn't want the last image of him in fans' minds to be one of him getting carted off a warning track in Kansas City.

18
CLOSING STATEMENTS

Mariano Rivera sees God's hand on his life. He believes God has blessed him and has orchestrated everything that has happened—the good *and* the bad. This attitude keeps the closer humble . . . and praying.

Mariano has seen God work through the losses in his life. Though the Yankees lost when he gave up the tying and winning runs to Arizona in Game 7 of the 2001 World Series, he knows that his teammate Enrique Wilson's life was saved when he changed his plane ticket. Mariano also knows that God will ultimately be glorified through his knee injury. He trusts the words of Romans 8:28: "We know that in all things God works for the good of those who love him, who have been called according to his purpose" (NIV). Mariano pays special attention to the phrase *all things* in that verse. He understands that God doesn't work just through the good things in life but that His purposes are also accomplished through

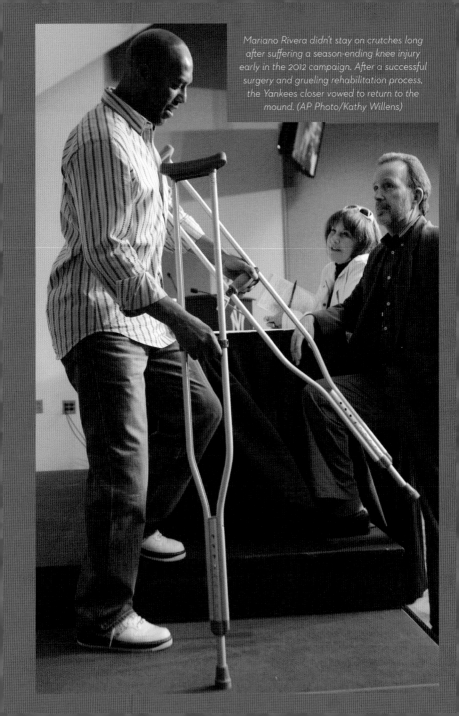

Mariano Rivera didn't stay on crutches long after suffering a season-ending knee injury early in the 2012 campaign. After a successful surgery and grueling rehabilitation process, the Yankees closer vowed to return to the mound. (AP Photo/Kathy Willens)

difficulty, through overcoming obstacles, and through pain.

Hours after Mariano tore the ACL in his right knee, reporters asked him if, as a man of faith, he wondered why the injury had occurred.

"No, I never will second guess that or question the Lord," Mariano answered emphatically. "It happened for a reason, and I just have to live with it."

Mariano's attention to detail has made him one of baseball's best pitchers. And doctors have said those same characteristics have helped him in his recovery from knee surgery.

Initially, doctors wanted to operate on Mariano's knee shortly after the injury. But during an examination, they discovered a blood clot in his calf. The reliever went on blood-thinning medication to dissolve the clot, which delayed the surgery. Never one to just sit around, Mariano worked with Dr. Keith Pyne and rehab specialist Ben Velazquez for a month before his surgery to strengthen the muscles around his knee.

"This is a very detailed guy, and he did everything right," Pyne said of Mariano's pre-surgery routine. "He strengthened. He got range of motion. He was very functional before surgery. I don't want to put a percentage on it, but he reduced recovery time by a lot."

Mariano received more good news after his June 12 surgery. Dr. David Altchek discovered that Mariano's ACL was partially, not fully, torn, as previously feared.

"My surgery was a success, it went perfectly," Mariano said on his Twitter account later that day. "I am looking forward to beginning my rehab soon. Thanks as always for your prayers."

Still a private person, Mariano has nonetheless become involved in social media, setting up Facebook and Twitter pages. More than 140,000 fans follow his Twitter posts.

A little more than a week after his surgery, Mariano went out to a Father's Day dinner with his family at Siro's, a restaurant in New York he co-owns. Diners gave him a standing ovation as he left, making a special day even better.

"This is the first time I've been home for Father's Day in twenty years," he said. "My recovery is going well, and I'm going to be back on the field as soon as possible."

Pyne didn't know Mariano before his injury, but three-hour rehab sessions four days a week allowed the two to become well acquainted with each other. Pyne had worked with more than eleven hundred athletes during his twenty-two years in the field, but he couldn't help but be impressed with the forty-two-year-old's extraordinary determination, flexibility, and athleticism.

"[Mariano] is special, in the top 10 percent of athletes I have worked with," Pyne said. "One great advantage he has is his lifestyle is very conducive to longevity. He eats well, prepares well. He is very cognizant of how to treat his body. That has put years onto his career. He is a special athlete with a special nervous system. He has great flexibility and joint mechanics. . . . But the most special thing about him is his cranium. He works and is focused on the task at hand. He attacks this like a professional."

Mariano has always credited his longevity in baseball to God's blessing and to living a clean, healthy lifestyle. He doesn't drink alcohol and has never done drugs. People won't find him out partying. After most games, he hurries home or to his hotel, and he's in bed about an hour after throwing his last pitch.

Fifty-Year-Old Pitcher?

During a September 2011 radio interview on "The Michael Kay Show" for ESPN New York, Mariano joked that he could pitch until he's fifty years old.

But maybe that's no joke. On April 17, 2012, Jamie Moyer of the Colorado Rockies became the oldest pitcher in major league history to win a game when he beat the San Diego Padres 5–3. Moyer pitched seven strong innings, relying on a 78-mile-per-hour fastball and a cutter. At forty-nine years and 150 days old, Moyer was eighty days older than Jack Quinn of the Brooklyn Dodgers, who previously held the record for the oldest pitcher to win a game after recording a victory in 1932. A month later, Moyer broke his own mark by winning another game for the Rockies, against Arizona.

The great Satchel Paige pitched three innings for the Kansas City Athletics in 1965. At the time, he was fifty-nine years, two months, and eighteen days old—making him the oldest pitcher ever to play a major league game.

In 2003, forty-two-year-old pitcher John Franco appeared in 38 games and recorded two saves for the New York Mets.

But the oldest player to save a game was Jack Quinn, who spent his final season with the Cincinnati Reds. On June 2, 1933, at the age of forty-nine, Quinn picked up a save against the Pittsburgh Pirates.

In 2010, Mariano was asked how much longer he wanted to pitch.

"If it's up to me, I might do it until my arm falls," he said.

"But I don't want to do my will. I want to do [God's] will, and He will lead me to the right path. If it's only one more year, or after this year, I don't know. I'm praying for the good Lord to direct me and help me to continue playing baseball."

The fact that Mariano takes care of himself and has avoided major arm problems—following his elbow surgery in 1992—makes many observers believe that the closer has a number of years as an effective pitcher ahead of him. And that's even after his 2012 knee injury.

Shortly after his surgery, reports circulated that Mariano might return near the end of the 2012 season. His rehabilitation was going better than expected, and the closer hoped to be ready by the playoffs.

In August, Mariano told reporters: "I want to pitch now. But that doesn't mean I will come back this year. It's that 1 percent we have to hope. . . . But at the same time you cannot push it. If you push it, you'll make a mistake. Instead of pitching this year, you won't pitch again next year. I have to be wise and make sure I do the right thing."

In mid-August, Mariano starting throwing long-toss sessions with the Yankees, but it was ultimately decided that he would focus on getting himself healthy for the 2013 season. Still, that didn't keep him away from the ballpark.

On October 10, Mariano returned to the mound at Yankee Stadium to throw out the ceremonial first pitch in Game 3 of the American League Division Series against the Baltimore Orioles.

As "Enter Sandman" blared over the sound system, No. 42 delivered a strike to backup catcher Chris Stewart. His team responded to the emotional boost by beating the Orioles 3–2 in 12 innings on its way to advancing to the next round of the playoffs.

Being back in the familiar confines of Yankee Stadium felt good to Mariano, but he was determined to return to his role as the team's everyday closer, even if that takes some time.

"I can't go down like this," Mariano says. "If it takes two, three, four, five, seven more [seasons], whatever it takes."

Although Mariano turned forty-three on November 29, 2012, Pyne said time is on his side.

"For me, there is biological age and chronological age," the doctor said. "I don't see Mariano Rivera's biological age as forty-two. He is mechanically and physically not a forty-two-year-old. He has the genetics of a much, much younger guy. This is not his last season. I cannot make the determination [of the exact date he will return]. But physically he will be able to do whatever it takes to pitch again."

Mariano's contract expired at the end of the 2012 season, but he signed a one-year, $10 million deal with New York on November 30, 2012, ensuring that he'll be back in pinstripes for 2013.

"Like I've been saying, I didn't want that [injury on the warning track] to be the last image," Mariano said in a statement. "But it wasn't an easy decision because there's more than just baseball with me. I have to consider my family and the church, too. But I feel like we have a great group of guys and a team that can compete for a championship. I'm not just coming back to play. I'm coming back to win."

No matter what the future holds for Mariano and the Yankees, one thing is certain in the minds of many fans: they'll never see a pitcher like Mo again.

"When you talk about the greatest relievers of all time, there's only one guy," Yankees teammate Mark Teixeira said. "That conversation begins and ends with Mo."

Mariano's longtime teammate Jorge Posada agreed. "Amazing that he's been able to do it with one pitch over and over again," the catcher said. "There will never be anybody like Mariano Rivera."

Mariano doesn't think much about how he'll be remembered in baseball history. He does hope, however, to be remembered for the impact he made on people and for the Lord.

"I don't pay too much attention to that," Mariano said when asked if he cared about being called the greatest relief pitcher who ever lived. "I just want to be the greatest person you've ever met. If I am, then I'm comfortable with that."

ABOUT THE AUTHORS

Jesse Florea has covered high school sports and written about professional athletes for more than twenty-seven years. He has written or co-written a dozen books, including *Playing with Purpose: Inside the Lives and Faith of the Major League's Top Players* (with Mike Yorkey and Joshua Cooley), *Linspired: The Jeremy Lin Story* (with Mike Yorkey), and *The One-Year Devos for Kids Who Love Sports* (with Joshua Cooley and Jeremy Jones).

Many of his sports stories appear in *Focus on the Family Clubhouse* (for boys and girls ages eight to twelve), a magazine that he's been the editor of for sixteen years. During his nineteen-year career at Focus on the Family, he's also worked as the editor of *Clubhouse Jr.* magazine (for children three to seven) and as associate editor of *Breakaway* magazine (teen boys). He has also edited the parenting edition of *Focus on the Family* magazine. He earned bachelor and master's degrees in communications from Wheaton College.

Jesse has two grown children and lives with his wife, Stephanie, in Colorado Springs.

Mike Yorkey, the author or co-author of more than seventy books, has written about sports all his life for a variety of national sports publications and book publishers. He has collaborated with Cleveland Browns quarterback Colt McCoy and his father, Brad, in *Growing Up Colt*; with San Francisco Giants pitcher Dave Dravecky (*Called Up* and *Play Ball*); with tennis stars Michael Chang *(Holding Serve)* and Betsy McCormack (*In His Court*); and with San Diego Chargers placekicker Rolf Benirschke (*Alive & Kicking*).

Believe: The Eric LeGrand StoryPlaying with Purpose: Inside the Lives and Faith of the Major League's Top PlayersPlaying with Purpose: Inside the Lives and Faith of Top NBA StarsPlaying with Purpose: Inside the Lives and Faith of the NFL's Top New Quarterbacks—Sam Bradford, Colt McCoy, and Tim Tebow Yorkey, who graduated from the University of Oregon's School of Journalism, is a former editor of *Focus on the Family* magazine and has also written for sports magazines such as *Skiing, Tennis*, and *Breakaway*. He is also a novelist, and his latest fiction effort is *Chasing Mona Lisa*, a World War II thriller he co-authored with Tricia Goyer.

Mike and his wife, Nicole, are the parents of two adult children, Andrea and Patrick. The Yorkeys make their home in Encinitas, California. Mike's website is www.mikeyorkey.com.

SOURCE MATERIAL

Chapter One

"For the first time in my career, I'm on the mound alone . . ." from "Mariano Rivera Sets New Saves Record" by Ian Begley, *ESPNNewYork.com*, September 19, 2011, and available at http://espn.go.com/new-york/mlb/story/_/id/6993396/new-york -yankees-mariano-rivera-sets-mlb-mark-602nd-save

"The whole organization, my whole teammates have been a pillar for me . . ." from "Mariano Rivera Gets 602 to Become All-Time Saves Leader" by Bryan Llenas, *Fox News Latino*, September 19, 2011, and available at http://latino.foxnews.com/latino/sports /2011/09/19/mariano-rivera-gets-number-602-to-become-all-time-saves-leader/

"I want to congratulate Mariano Rivera on setting the all-time saves record . . ." Begley, "Mariano Rivera Sets New Saves Record."

"Yes, it does. It does make me uncomfortable, because I don't like to talk about myself . . ." from "The Michael Kay Show," ESPN New York (1050 AM) podcast, September 16, 2011, and available at http://espn.go.com/new-york/radio /archive?id=2693958

"I'm thankful to my wife, my kids, my family, the organization, my teammates . . ." from "Mariano Rivera, Already a Yankees Legend, Becomes All-Time Saves Leader" by Marc Craig, *The Star-Ledger,* September 19, 2011, and available at http://www .nj.com/yankees/index.ssf/2011/09/yankees_closer_mariano_rivera_12.html

Chapter Two

"He's been [chasing fly balls] and no one ever said a word" from "Rivera Hurts Knee; Career May Be Over" by David Waldstein, NYTimes.com, May 3, 2012, and available at http://www.nytimes.com/2012/05/04/sports/baseball/yankees-mariano -rivera-injured-during-batting-practice.html?pagewanted=all

"I got myself between the grass and the dirt, couldn't pull my leg up, and twisted my knee . . ." from postgame interview on YESNetwork.com, May 3, 2012, and available at http://www.youtube.com/watch?v=uZlpgUbEZw4

"I'm coming back" from "No More Mo?" by Joe Sheehan, *Sports Illustrated*, May 14, 2012, 32.

Chapter Three

"That is my miracle pitch . . ." from "Mariano Rivera's Cutter 'The Miracle Pitch,'" interview with Pastor Dewey Friedel, courtesy Trinity Broadcasting Network, and available at http://www.youtube.com/watch?v=L0tTLssCKZU

"We were trying to make the pitch stay straighter . . ." from "Mariano Saves" by Tom Verducci, *Sports Illustrated*, October 5, 2009, and available at http://sportsillustrated.cnn.com/vault/article/magazine/MAG1160757/index.htm

"[Mariano] needs to pitch in a higher league, if there is one . . ." from "Mariano Rivera's a True Yankee, Almost Mythical in His Dominance" by Joe Posnanski, SI.com, July 2, 2009, and available at http://sportsillustrated.cnn.com/2009/writers/joe_posnanski/07/01/rivera/index.html

"When I broke in I could count on one hand the number of guys who threw it . . ." from "This Is the Game Changer," by Albert Chen, *Sports Illustrated*, June 13, 2011, and available at http://sportsillustrated.cnn.com/vault/article/magazine/MAG1187105/index.htm

"Look at Mo's delivery, look at how he repeats it . . ." from "Mariano Rivera Pitches in 1,000th Game for Yanks and Has a Lot of Mo" by Bob Klapisch, *The Record*, May 28, 2011, and available at http://www.post-gazette.com/pg/11148/1150003-63-0.stm?cmpid=sports.xml

"You can't see the spin on it . . ." from "This Is the Game Changer," by Albert Chen, *Sports Illustrated*, June 13, 2011, and available at http://sportsillustrated.cnn.com/vault/article/magazine/MAG1187105/index.htm

"I'm a thousand percent. A thousand percent sure . . ." Verducci "Mariano Saves."

"My mental approach is simple: Get three outs as quick as possible . . ." from "Mariano Saves" by Tom Verducci

Chapter Four

"If the pressure is so much that it doesn't allow you to do your job . . ." from "Yanks' Rivera Continues to Learn" by Mel Antonen, *USA Today*, October 9, 2006, and available at http://www.usatoday.com/sports/soac/2006-10-09-rivera_x.htm

"If I doubted myself, I wouldn't be doing this . . ." from "The Michael Kay Show," ESPN New York (1050 AM) podcast, April 26, 2012, and available at http://espn .go.com/blog/new-york/yankees/post/_/id/33006/podcast-mariano-rivera

"I don't call them blown saves . . ." from "The Michael Kay Show," ESPN New York (1050 AM) podcast, September 16, 2011, and available at http://espn.go.com/new -york/radio/archive?id=2693958

"When God takes control of everything, he's inside of you and He brings you strength . . ." from "Baseball; Love of God Outweighs Love of the Game" by Jack Curry, *New York Times*, December 10, 1999, and available at http://www.nytimes. com/1999/12/10/sports/baseball-love-of-god-outweighs-love-of-the-game.html

"I feel like it's just me and the catcher . . ." from "Richard Gere Interviews Mariano Rivera" by Richard Gere, *Gotham,* May 3, 2012, and available at http://gotham -magazine.com/personalities/articles/richard-gere-interviews-yankees-star-mariano-rivera -on-retirement-rumors-and-life-off-the-field

"Every time before I throw my first pitch, I am praying . . ." Gere "Richard Gere Interviews Mariano Rivera."

"I don't get nervous . . ." from "Yanks' Rivera Continues to Learn" by Mel Antonen, *USA Today,* October 9, 2006, and available at http://www.usatoday.com/sports/soac/2006-10 -09-rivera_x.htm

"Since I was a little one, I was real competitive . . ." from "Richard Gere Interviews Mariano Rivera."

"He's a trip in here during the game—screaming, yelling, cheering, rooting . . ." from "Yanks' Closer Also Serves as Mentor and Counselor" by David Waldstein, the *New York Times,* September 14, 2011, and available at http://www.nytimes.com/2011/09/15 /sports/baseball/to-yankees-teammates-rivera-is-just-as-valuable-in-private.html?_r=0

"I love everything about pitching . . ." from "Mariano Saves" by Tom Verducci, *Sports Illustrated,* October 5, 2009, and available at http://sportsillustrated.cnn.com/vault/article /magazine/MAG1160757/index.htm

Chapter Five

"My childhood was wonderful . . ." from "Modern Yankee Heroes: From Humble Beginnings, Mariano Rivera Becomes Greatest Closer in MLB History" by Christian Red, *New York Daily News*, March 13, 2010, and available at http://articles.nydailynews .com/2010-03-13/sports/27058930_1_puerto-caimito-cardboard-cousin

"Extremely hard . . ." from "Modern Yankee Heroes: From Humble Beginnings, Mariano Rivera Becomes Greatest Closer in MLB History" by Christian Red, *New York Daily News*, March 13, 2010, and available at http://articles.nydailynews.com/2010-03-13 /sports/27058930_1_puerto-caimito-cardboard-cousin

"From my father's side, I got the strength, the mental toughness, the heart, the courage," from "Richard Gere Interviews Mariano Rivera" by Richard Gere, *Gotham,* May 3, 2012, and available at http://gotham-magazine.com/personalities/articles/richard-gere -interviews-yankees-star-mariano-rivera-on-retirement-rumors-and-life-off-the-field

"The piece of my mother I have [is] the gentleness, the worries, making sure everybody is okay," Gere.

Chapter Six

"As a scout, you're signing players to get to the big leagues, not Double-A or Triple-A" from "Modern Yankee Heroes: From Humble Beginnings, Mariano Rivera Becomes Greatest Closer in MLB History" by Christian Red, *New York Daily News*, March 13, 2010, and available at http://articles.nydailynews.com/2010-03-13/sports/27058930_1 _puerto-caimito-cardboard-cousin

"I gave him good marks in his fielding and throwing . . ." Red "Modern Yankee Heroes.

"I wasn't nervous . . ." from "Scout Saw Effortless Ability in Rivera" by Jack Curry, the *New York Times*, July 6, 2009, and available at http://www.nytimes.com/2009/07/06 /sports/baseball/06scout.html

"The radar wasn't really being lit up . . ." Red "Modern Yankee Heroes.

"Usually a player prepares for years . . ." from *Mariano Rivera* by Judith Levin (New York: Checkmark Books, 2008), 18.

Chapter Seven
"My first year when I was in Tampa and my second year in North Carolina, it was no English . . ." from "Richard Gere Interviews Mariano Rivera" by Richard Gere, *Gotham*, May 3, 2012, and available at http://gotham-magazine.com/personalities/articles/richard-gere-interviews-yankees-star-mariano-rivera-on-retirement-rumors-and-life-off-the-field

"This guy is our best outfielder" from *Mariano Rivera* by Judith Levin (New York: Checkmark Books, 2008), 22.

"After Mo had surgery, when we were in the minor leagues, he was on a pitch count" from "Modern Yankee Heroes: From Humble Beginnings, Mariano Rivera Becomes Greatest Closer in MLB History" by Christian Red, *New York Daily News*, March 13, 2010, and available at http://articles.nydailynews.com/2010-03-13/sports/27058930_1_puerto-caimito-cardboard-cousin

"Every time I was going through a hard time, somebody was there to help . . ." from "The Secret of Mariano Rivera's Success" by Peter Schiller, baseballreflections.com, November 7, 2009, and available at http://baseballreflections.com/2009/11/07/the-secret-of-mariano-riveras-success/

"I realized the Lord wanted a relationship with me . . . " from "Athlete Testimonies and available at http://www.sportsspectrum.com/resources/testimonies/?by_name=Mariano+Rivera

Chapter Eight
"I know what people were probably thinking then . . ." from *Mariano Rivera* by Judith Levin (New York: Checkmark Books, 2008), 30.

Chapter Nine
"I didn't pick that song . . ." from "Keeping the Faith" by Dave Hollander, *SI.com*, May 27, 2005, and available at http://sportsillustrated.cnn.com/2005/writers/dave_hollander/05/27/mariano.rivera/index.html

"After Mo is done, we won't use that for anyone else . . ." from "Cue the 'Sandman': Mariano, Song Synonymous" by Bryan Hoch, MLB.com, September 15, 2011, and available at http://newyork.yankees.mlb.com/news/article.jsp?ymd=20110911&content_id=24568646

"When I think of 1996, I think of Mariano Rivera," from *Mariano Rivera* by Judith Levin (New York: Checkmark Books, 2008), page 53.

"To me that was a crazy move . . ." from "Richard Gere Interviews Mariano Rivera" by Richard Gere, *Gotham,* May 3, 2012, and available at http://gotham-magazine.com /personalities/articles/richard-gere-interviews-yankees-star-mariano-rivera-on-retirement -rumors-and-life-off-the-field

"The harder I tried, the tougher it got . . ." from "Yanks' Rivera Continues to Learn" by Mel Antonen, *USA Today*, October 9, 2006, and available at http://www.usatoday.com /sports/soac/2006-10-09-rivera_x.htm

Chapter Ten
"I never will . . ." from "The Confidence Man" by Buster Olney, *New York Magazine*, May 21, 2005, and available at http://nymag.com/nymetro/news/sports/features/9375/index2 .html

"I was thanking God for everything" from *Mariano Rivera* by Judith Levin (New York: Checkmark Books, 2008), 64.

"I am the one who has you here" from "Baseball; Love of God Outweighs Love of the Game" by Jack Curry, *New York Times*, December 10, 1999, and available at http://www .nytimes.com/1999/12/10/sports/baseball-love-of-god-outweighs-love-of-the-game.html

"We all were MVPs . . ." from "Just Like Wetteland," the Associated Press, October 28, 1999, and available at http://sportsillustrated.cnn.com/baseball/mlb/1999/postseason /world_series/news/1999/10/27/rivera_mvp_ap/

"He's the best . . ." Associated Press "Just Like Wetteland."

"That meant that the only reason I'm here is because He's my strength . . ." Curry "Baseball; Love of God Outweighs Love of the Game."

"Inside of me, I'm thinking four more years," from "Baseball; Love of God Outweighs Love of the Game" by Jack Curry, *New York Times*, December 10, 1999, and available at http://www.nytimes.com/1999/12/10/sports/baseball-love-of-god-outweighs-love-of-the-game.html

Chapter Eleven
"The most crucial factor and the greatest reason the Yankees are three-time champions is Rivera . . . ." from "Closing Thoughts: Rivera Remains the Infallible One" by Jack Curry, the *New York Times*, October 29, 2000, and available at http://www.nytimes. com/2000/10/29/sports/baseball-subway-series-closing-thoughts-rivera-remains-the -infallible-one.html?pagewanted=all&src=pm

"The core group, winning four World Series out of five years, in this day and age . . ." from "Vic-Torre," CNNSI.com, October 26, 2000, and available at http://sportsillustrated.cnn.com/baseball/mlb/2000/world_series/news/2000/10/26/yankees_mets_game5_ap/

"Mr. George, I learned a lot from that man . . ." from "Richard Gere Interviews Mariano Rivera" by Richard Gere, *Gotham*, May 3, 2012, and available at http://gotham-magazine.com/personalities/articles/richard-gere-interviews-yankees-star-mariano-rivera-on-retirement-rumors-and-life-off-the-field

"I'm glad we lost the World Series . . ." from "The Confidence Man" by Buster Olney, *New York Magazine*, May 21, 2005, and available at http://nymag.com/nymetro/news/sports/features/9375/index2.html

"The most difficult part of my day was leaving my family, knowing they are still in pain . . ." from *Mariano Rivera* by Judith Levin (New York: Checkmark Books, 2008), 94.

Chapter Twelve
"He's always got a smile on his face, and people don't see that . . ." from "Yankees Players Awed by Rivera" by Mark Feinsand, *mlb.com*, July 16, 2006, and available at http://newyork.yankees.mlb.com/news/article.jsp?ymd=20060627&content_id=1525776&vkey=news_nyy&fext=.jsp&c_id=nyy

"He's like my brother . . ." from "Modern Yankee Heroes: From Humble Beginnings, Mariano Rivera Becomes Greatest Closer in MLB History" by Christian Red, *New York Daily News*, March 13, 2010, and available at http://articles.nydailynews.com/2010-03-13/sports/27058930_1_puerto-caimito-cardboard-cousin

"Mariano was my answer . . ." Feinsand "Yankees Players Awed by Rivera"

"I cannot move without his direction" from "Not Done Yet" by Bob Bellone, *Sports Spectrum,* Fall 2010, and available at http://www.sportsspectrum.com/articles/2012/05/04/not-done-yet/

"Mo reaches out to everybody . . ." Feinsand "Yankees Players Awed by Rivera"

"It's a hard road in the minor leagues . . ." Bellone "Not Done Yet"

"I don't know if we'll ever see it again . . ." from "Mariano Rivera gets 600th save" by Andrew Marchand, ESPNNewYork.com, September 14, 2011, and available at http://m.espn.go.com/mlb/story?w=1b0rl&storyId=6968238&i=TOP&wjb=

"You're seeing the greatest closer of all time . . ." from "Mariano Saves" by Tom Verducci, *Sports Illustrated*, October 5, 2009, and available at http://sportsillustrated.cnn.com/vault /article/magazine/MAG1160757/index.htm

"He's better than any guy I have ever seen . . ." Feinsand "Yankees Players Awed by Rivera"

"He was telling me about things he wanted me to do to help the team . . ." from "Yanks' Closer Also Serves as Mentor and Counselor" by David Waldstein, the *New York Times*, September 14, 2011, and available at http://www.nytimes.com/2011/09/15/sports /baseball/to-yankees-teammates-rivera-is-just-as-valuable-in-private.html?_r=0

"He'll call me into the trainer's room and say, 'What are you doing?' . . ." Waldstein "Yanks' Closer Also Serves as Mentor and Counselor."

"Equally as impressive as 600 [saves] is what he's done in here for everyone as a leader . . ." Waldstein "Yanks' Closer Also Serves as Mentor and Counselor."

Chapter Thirteen
"I think everyone who knows him feels the same way" from "Civil Mariano Garners Respect Like No Other," by Peter Gammons, MLB.com, May 4, 2012, and available at http://newyork.yankees.mlb.com/news/article.jsp?ymd=20120504&content _id=30366282&vkey=news_mlb&c_id=mlb

"If you talk to him at an All-Star Game, it's like talking to somebody who just got called up . . ." from "Mariano Saves" by Tom Verducci, *Sports Illustrated*, October 5, 2009, and available at http://sportsillustrated.cnn.com/vault/article/magazine/MAG1160757/index .htm

"I don't wait for people to give me respect . . ." Verducci "Mariano Saves."

"Being the only one carrying the number right now, and forever, this means a lot to me," from "Yankees' Mariano Rivera Is the Last No. 42" by Harvey Araton, the *New York Times*, April 14, 2010, and available at http://www.nytimes.com/2010/04/15/sports /baseball/15rivera.html?_r=0

"I've been very pleased that he is the last one to wear Jack's number . . ." Araton "Yankees' Mariano Rivera Is the Last No. 42."

"If we had Rivera in Atlanta, we would have won about three or four World Series . . ." from "Closing Thoughts: Rivera Remains the Infallible One" Curry

"To have a guy like him is a tremendous psychological advantage . . ." Curry "Closing Thoughts: Rivera Remains the Infallible One."

"I believe that one will never go wrong treating people the way you want them to treat you," Gammons "Civil Mariano Garners Respect Like No Other."

Chapter Fourteen

"The foundation started like this . . ." from "Richard Gere Interviews Mariano Rivera" by Richard Gere, *Gotham*, May 3, 2012, and available at http://gotham-magazine.com /personalities/articles/richard-gere-interviews-yankees-star-mariano-rivera-on-retirement -rumors-and-life-off-the-field

"You go into villages where they don't have anything . . ." from "Steiner Sports Interview on Charity Work" by Brandon Steiner and available at http://www .themarianoriverafoundation.org/#!video/cdxq

"I want to present this trophy to the true saviors, the true closers" from "Rivera Wins Relief Award and Gives It to 'True Closers'" by Rafael Hermoso, *New York Times*, January 28, 2002, and available at http://www.nytimes.com/2002/01/28/sports/baseball-rivera -wins-relief-award-and-gives-it-to-true-closers.html

"I remember what the firefighters did in 2001 . . ." Steiner "Steiner Sports Interview on Charity Work."

"Scholarships give opportunities to kids and families who don't have much . . ." Steiner "Steiner Sports Interview on Charity Work."

"In the foundation, we try to spread out our efforts as much as we can . . ." from "Steiner Sports Interview on Charity Work" Steiner.

"Winning is the most important thing in my life, after breathing . . ." from "George Steinbrenner: In His Own Words" *SI.com*, July 13, 2010, and available at http:// sportsillustrated.cnn.com/2010/baseball/mlb/07/13/steinbrenner.quotes/index.html

Chapter Fifteen

"Mr. George, he gave me the opportunity, and he gave me the chance . . ." from "A Long Goodbye to an 85-Year Run" by Tyler Kepner, *New York Times*, September 21, 2008, and available at http://www.nytimes.com/2008/09/22/sports/baseball/22yankees .html?pagewanted=all&_r=0

"It's wonderful to be able to play with those bunch of guys . . ." from "Six Games, Five Rings, Four Yankees" by Bryan Hoch, *MLB.com*, November 5, 2009, and available at http://newyork.yankees.mlb.com/news/article.jsp?ymd=20091104&content_id=7620796&vkey=ps2009news&fext=.jsp&c_id=mlb

"They're guys who really showed you how to be a New York Yankee . . ." from "Jeter, Pettitte, Rivera and Posada: The 2009 WS Was Special to the 'Humble 4'" by Harold Friend, *BleacherReport.com*, March 27, 2012, and available at http://bleacherreport.com/articles/1121094-jeter-pettitte-rivera-and-posada-the-2009-ws-was-special-to-the-humble-four

"I never forgot, but when you're in there you know how much you missed it . . ." Hoch "Six Games, Five Rings, Four Yankees."

Chapter Sixteen
"We have a lot of goals that we want to fulfill, but the main goal right now is to restore the church" from "Yankees Closer Rivera Helps Save a Century-Old Church" by Jeff Schapiro, *Christian Post*, June 29, 2011, and available at http://www.christianpost.com/news/yankees-closer-rivera-helps-save-a-century-old-church-51696/

"Back to its former luster, and with its original purpose, as a house of worship," Schapiro "Yankees Closer Rivera Helps Save a Century-Old Church."

"I love this glove . . ." from "Mariano Rivera Talks about His First Glove," video interview with Brandon Steiner, uploaded September 21, 2011, and available at youtube.com/watch?v=kTJnkFjFBNE

"We have a lot of goals to work with the youth . . ." from "Yankees Pitcher to Open Church" by Danielle De Souza, *New Rochelle Patch*, June 28, 2011, and available at http://newrochelle.patch.com/articles/yankees-pitcher-to-open-church

"The game is my job, but life continues . . ." Schapiro "Yankees Closer Rivera Helps Save a Century-Old Church."

"It's not just reaching into your pocket to give back . . ." from "Steiner Sports Interview on Charity Work" by Brandon Steiner and available at http://www.themarianoriverafoundation.org/#!video/cdxq

Chapter Seventeen

"He has no fear of failure . . ." from "Strikeouts by the Boatload" by Michael Bamberger, *Sports Illustrated*, March 24, 1997, and available at http://sportsillustrated.cnn.com/vault /article/magazine/MAG1009676/3/index.htm

"Let's face it . . ." from "Mariano Saves" by Tom Verducci, *Sports Illustrated*, October 5, 2009, and available at http://sportsillustrated.cnn.com/vault/article/magazine /MAG1160757/index.htm

"That comes from God, having the ability to perform . . ." from "World Baseball Classic Pool D: San Juan," an interview with Mariano Rivera by ASAP Sports, March 7, 2009, and available at http://www.asapsports.com/show_interview.php?id=54723

"Hollander: If Jesus was a major league pitcher, would He be a starter, middle reliever, or a closer . . ." from "Keeping the Faith" by Dave Hollander, *SI.com,* May 27, 2005, and available at http://sportsillustrated.cnn.com/2005/writers/ dave_hollander/05/27/mariano.rivera/index.html

"There's no doubt . . ." from "Mariano Rivera, Already a Yankees Legend, Becomes All-Time Saves Leader" by Marc Craig, *The Star-Ledger*, September 19, 2011, and available at http://www.nj.com/yankees/index.ssf/2011/09/yankees_closer_mariano_rivera_12.html

Chapter Eighteen

"No, I never will second guess that or question the Lord . . ." from postgame interview on YESNetwork.com, May 3, 2012, and available at http://www.youtube.com /watch?v=uZlpgUbEZw4

"This is a very detailed guy, and he did everything right . . ." from "Rehab Doctor: Rivera Could Pitch for Yankees This Season" by Joel Sherman, *New York Post*, July 10, 2012, and available at http://www.nypost.com/p/sports/yankees/mo_surprise _ogf4OfTJP19NBdvzfDZPQK

"My surgery was a success, it went perfectly . . ." from Mariano Rivera's Twitter account, June 12, 2012, and available at https://twitter.com/MarianoRivera

"This is the first time I've been home for Father's Day in twenty years . . ." from "Cheers for Rivera," *New York Post*, June 20, 2012, and available at http://www.nypost.com/p /pagesix/cheers_for_rivera_ClNxoPVGEaPAKV5K0l1qFM

"[Mariano] is special, in the top 10 percent of athletes I have worked with," Sherman "Rehab Doctor: Rivera Could Pitch for Yankees This Season."

"If it's up to me, I might do it until my arm falls . . ." from "Not Done Yet" by Bob Bellone, *Sports Spectrum*, Fall 2010, and available at http://www.sportsspectrum.com /articles/2012/05/04/not-done-yet/

"I want to pitch now. But that doesn't mean I will come back this year . . ." from "Mariano Rivera Working Hard," Associated Press, August 10, 2012, and available at http://espn.go.com/new-york/mlb/story/_/id/8257372/mariano-rivera-new-york -yankees-working-hard-return-injury

"I can't go down like this . . ." from "Yankees Closer Mariano Rivera Has Blood Clot in Calf" CBS News/Associated Press, May 9, 2012, and available at http://www.cbsnews .com/8301-400_162-57431253/yankees-closer-mariano-rivera-has-blood-clot-in-calf/

"For me there is biological age and chronological age . . ." Sherman "Rehab Doctor: Rivera Could Pitch for Yankees This Season."

"Like I've been saying, I didn't want that [injury on the warning track] to be the last image," from "Yankees finalize one-year, $10M deal with Rivera" by Associated Press, November 30, 2012, and available at http://sportsillustrated.cnn.com/2012/baseball/ mlb/11/30/yankees-rivera.ap/index.html

"When you talk about the greatest relievers of all time, there's only one guy . . ." from "Mariano Rivera: Saving with Grace" by Kevin Baxter, *Los Angeles Times*, September 17, 2011, and available at http://articles.latimes.com/2011/sep/17/sports/la-sp-0918-down -the-line-20110918

"Amazing that he's been able to do it with one pitch over and over again . . ." from "Modern Yankee Heroes: From Humble Beginnings, Mariano Rivera Becomes Greatest Closer in MLB History" by Christian Red, *New York Daily News*, March 13, 2010, and available at http://articles.nydailynews.com/2010-03-13/sports/27058930_1_puerto -caimito-cardboard-cousin

"I don't pay too much attention to that . . ." from "The Michael Kay Show," ESPN New York (1050 AM) podcast, September 16, 2011, and available at http://espn.go.com/new -york/radio/archive?id=2693958

For more great stories of
faith in sport,
check out the
Playing with Purpose
Series!

PLAYING WITH PURPOSE: BASKETBALL

Meet the "dream team" of talented NBA players with fascinating faith stories, including 2012 sensation Jeremy Lin of the New York Knicks. ISBN 978-1-61626-489-5

PLAYING WITH PURPOSE: BASEBALL

Meet the "starting lineup" of talented major league players with fascinating faith stories, including Albert Pujols, Josh Hamilton, Mariano Rivera, and 2011 Cy Young Winner Clayton Kershaw. ISBN 978-1-61626-490-1

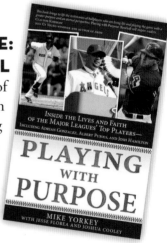

Available wherever Christian books are sold.